SPIRITUAL QUEST

Discovering Your
Higher Self Through Love

Sally DeMasi

Copyright © 2017 by Sally DeMasi

All rights reserved

Printed in the United States of America

No part of this work may be reproduced
in any form without the written
permission of the copyright owner.

Email sallydemasi4@gmail.com
PO Box 32
McCall, ID 83638

For more information about this book or the
author, visit www.SurvivalSpiritualQuest.com
or sallydemasi4.wixsite.com/quest

Paperback ISBN: 978-0-9967033-3-8
Electronic ISBN: 978-0-9967033-2-1

Disclaimer: Although the author and publisher have
made every effort to ensure that the information
in this book was correct at press time, the author
and publisher do not assume and hereby disclaim
any liability to any party for any loss, damage,
or disruption caused by errors or omissions,
whether such errors or omissions result from
negligence, accident, or any other cause.

Cover design by Jenn Reese, Tiger Bright Studios

This book is dedicated to my daughter, Nicole, my shining light who has gently guided me on my search for spirituality through her love.

Our deepest fear is not that we are inadequate.

> Our deepest fear is that we are
> powerful beyond measure.

> It is our light, not our darkness,
> that most frightens us.

We ask ourselves, who am I to be brilliant,
gorgeous, talented, and fabulous?

> Actually, who are you not to be?

> You are a child of God. Your playing
> small doesn't serve the world.

There's nothing enlightened about shrinking so
that other people won't feel insecure around you.

> We were born to make manifest the
> glory of God that is within us.

> It's not just in some of us: it's in everyone.

> And as we let our own light shine,
> we unconsciously give other people
> permission to do the same.

As we are liberated from our own fear, our
presence automatically liberates others.

MARIANNE WILLIAMSON
*A Return to Love: Reflections on the
Principle of A Course in Miracles*

Move out of your comfort zone. You can only grow if you are willing to feel awkward and uncomfortable when you try something new.

Brian Tracy

How different our lives are when we really know what is deeply important to us, and keeping that picture in mind, we manage ourselves each day to be and to do what really matters most.

Stephen R. Covey

A ship in harbor is safe, but that is not what ships are built for.

John A. Shedd

Life is a great big canvas, and you should throw all the paint on it you can.

Danny Kaye

Embarking on the spiritual journey is like getting into a very small boat and setting out on the ocean to search for unknown lands.

Pema Chodron

So many of our dreams at first seem impossible, then they seem improbable, and then, when we summon the will, they soon become inevitable.

Christopher Reeve

Contents

Introduction: The Awakening *1*

Chapter 1: Nature *13*
Chapter 2: Religion and Belief Systems *35*
Chapter 3: Angels Among Us. *57*
Chapter 4: Death and Living with Purpose. *75*
Chapter 5: Vision Quest. *103*
Chapter 6: Forgiveness. *123*
Chapter 7: The Now *137*
Chapter 8: Love, What Binds and Makes Us Human . . . *159*
Chapter 9: Fear *201*
Chapter 10: Surrender Gives Happiness with Gratitude . . *217*
Chapter 11: New Beginnings. *241*

Acknowledgments *259*
My Research *261*
About the Author. *265*

Introduction
The Awakening

There is no certainty; there is only adventure.

Roberto Assagioli

In 1992, before I fully embarked on the search for where spirituality fit in my life, I set off on a one hundred mile, arduous journey down the Amazon River. While there was a spiritual drive buried inside waiting for release, I was just dipping my toe in the smooth waters of exploration, wondering how they might merge into one significant body of understanding. Little did I suspect when departing my empty, numb, technology-directed life that a vacation across the ocean would germinate a seed within me, inciting a growth into the spiritual person I am today.

Unknowingly, my guide, Javier, became responsible for an accident of fate as we moved down the slow-moving, murky Amazon. September is the end of their winter season. With less precipitation, the water level was so low that many of the tributaries had dried up. The water was difficult to navigate, and we confronted dangerous encumbrances ready to snag and tip our boat. It was hell.

The stagnant river hampered what we had expected would be an easy paddle on the water, and the camping also wasn't without its troubles. One night we set up on a low sand barge where insects bit every part of my body, imparting welts. We sought cover in our tents from the pelting rain and violent sparks of lightning, which seemed directly aimed at us. The skies opened up, releasing a violent torrent of water that threatened to flood our encampment, just eighteen inches above the now angry river, and possibly carry us to destruction.

Had we angered the Gods? My trip manifested the truth. I became violently ill from my guide's dishwashing technique. Every night when we camped at sunset, he'd vigorously scrub our dishes with a bar of Ivory soap, using his grimy, sweaty hands. Then he'd rinse the dishes in the bacteria-infested river.

My stomach raged. The insect bites became infected. Worms entered my feet and moved through my body. I reminded myself that I had embarked on this trip to find courage, but now I had just one wish—I could drift to heaven, if one existed?

Although very sick, I stubbornly moved on after the Amazon paddle alone to explore the south of Peru, ending at Lake Titicaca, a spiritual energy-charged vortex. Next I planned on tackling Machu Picchu; it was something I had to do. Actually, I felt driven to keep going, though I wasn't quite sure why. At that point, I had not yet named what I was seeking, but this experience marked the beginning of my search for a personal connection to the universe and a desire to understand how this discovery might guide me to be the person I was meant to be.

In pain, I landed at the Inca Manco Capac International Airport and drove south to the small town of Puno. My taxi driver somehow intuitively understood my internal state. Knowing that I needed to return home immediately, he appeared at my hotel the next day and assisted me by making the arrangements. So with extreme sadness, I complied.

This "guide" secured a ticket for me out of Peru within twenty-four hours (very unusual to obtain a flight on such short notice). On the drive to the airport, we talked about very personal topics—our connection to the universe, a higher being, and what might lie ahead for each of us. At first, I thought it was too personal a conversation to be having with a stranger, and then it felt more comfortable, acceptable even, as I began to expand my vision of the spirit world. When he deposited me at the airport, I was so dehydrated and full of infection, I could barely stand, hear or even think. I felt immense appreciation for this man's efforts and protection.

Letting go of visiting Machu Picchu, a major goal of this trip, I returned to the United States. I took a month off from work to heal and used all the internal and external medicine my doctor had prescribed. "You are one lucky lady that you lived through this," she said. I was.

That fateful trip to South America introduced me to my quest as a spiritual traveler. Looking back, I failed to reach my destination—these surreal ancient ruins, ceremonial sites and temples, all nestled on top of a mountain—because it was simply *not my time*. Not my time to visit such a spiritual, energy-charged location because I didn't understand enough about spiritual concepts and how to consume this information.

My experience with the taxi driver, who rescued me through his sixth-sense intuition, made me wonder how this occurred. It ignited my imagination and stimulated possibilities as I learned more about the spiritual world. *What is possible in life? How do I uncover the unknown?*

Again, driven by a force to complete my abandoned trip, I rescheduled a visit to Machu Picchu four years later. This time armed with more knowledge of the spiritual world.

Arriving in Lima, I immediately flew to the hilly, cobble-stoned city of Cusco, eleven thousand feet in the clouds. It's an interesting city. Once part of the Inca Empire, Cusco was conquered by the Spanish who then ruled this territory, imparting their stunning colonial architecture.

Incredulous, I became sick. This time I had altitude sickness, different than what I'd had before but with some similar intestinal symptoms. Although uncomfortable, I was determined to visit Machu Picchu.

I pushed myself to explore Cusco for a day despite an upset stomach and a pounding headache, which no amount of coca tea or water could alleviate. My discomfort continued until I eventually had to relinquish my visit to Argentina and, again, fly home before my trip's scheduled completion in order to recover. But I would not leave before I had a chance to experience Machu Picchu.

Although ill and uncomfortable, and now battling a nasty flu, this very tenacious voyager was determined to visit this primitive Inca civilization and to finally immerse herself in the city of the Gods. Waking at 3:00 am for the first train up the mountain, I boarded the Vistadome with butterflies in my stomach. As the train's wheels negotiated curvy twists and gains in altitude, the green of the jungle foliage rushing by calmed me. We were heading to the base of the majestic mountains that surrounded this revered, once-hidden society of mystical power.

I felt such wonder among these ruins and uncovered a connection with the universe that I had never suspected resided within me. I wrote about this discovery in my book *Courage Quest*.

Once in this revered place, my life force pulsed as I ran up and down the ruins taking photos. Finally I came upon a stone ledge built eons ago and stopped. I stopped trying to bring back images for others and instead immersed myself in the spirits there. They filled my heart and soul, releasing tremendous gratitude for all I possessed now in this place.

I could feel the ones who had lived here as I sat on these ancient stones. The cramps and sickness left my body, allowing me to breathe in the depth of this past civilization's rituals, vibrations and spirit in the present moment. I embraced this experience, it was only for me. I felt reborn. As I rested on that ancient rock, a place of solace, I realized others had also rested in this spot to relax in the sun, to revitalize. That knowledge filled me with tranquility. It was a peace I had longed for, yet had no compass to find until I absorbed all in this moment, in this divine place offering the gift of a mind-body spiritual connection.

What I gained that day always astounds me. Everything I had learned over the preceding four years was preparation for the receiving in the mountains of Machu Picchu. During those previous years, I explored meditation, different religions and yoga; those experiences introduced me to the deep pure forces here that I could align with.

No longer would I strive to relay my adventures, bragging to others where I had explored in the world. In that moment, I soaked up the reverence and beauty and, most of all, the power of change. I was like a sprouting flower that had lain dormant an eternity.

What happened in that valley that transformed me? What drove me to return to a country where I had previously been so ill? Maybe it was now my time for discovery and to begin moving forward on this road into the unknown.

That sacred valley is considered one of the most energetically charged places on earth with robust spiritual undertones. It is surrounded by twenty thousand-foot, glacier-topped Andean peaks that are considered powerful deities by the spiritual community. This force immensely redirected my life. Did sickness attempt to get my attention?

Once home, I began my inner spiritual search in earnest. I tackled questions that I shared with others. What does this enchanted word *spirituality* mean? Why are we here and how do we learn from our mistakes? Why must we let go of our desires to have them materialize? How can we control time and hone our attention to increase effectiveness in our daily lives, especially when the days seem to move so fast? How do we find ways to break free of our long lists of must-dos and contribute to the world, healing ourselves and others? How do we find joy in the face of suffering? How do we overcome obstacles of anger, stress, fear, grief, illness and death?

I asked people, even those I didn't know, what they were searching for in their spirualty. Many were at a loss for words. Some thought more deeply but then said that they couldn't answer at this time, had no idea what to base their answers on or just didn't want to consider it right now. Many stated that their belief in God, and Jesus, if they were Christian, provided all the answers and guidance they required. They weren't searching.

But there was still the issues of those who did have a wish to search.

One person told me that spirituality and love are the same. This was exactly what I had learned since embarking on this journey. We search for answers about how love is relevant to our life, or we don't. I continued to explore.

For me, at this juncture, spirituality means a set of convictions; my personal guide of tools and beliefs that influence the way I currently live my life. Spirituality is my foundation. I draw strength from the celestial world, which includes guides and angels, so I can respect and help others (people, animals and our planet) in a simple, personal way and live with joy, serenity and gratitude. My spirituality radiates from my heart, my soul. I am godlike, an important grain in the universe. My spirituality is my relationship to nature.

This esoteric form of an individual relationship with a world beyond our earthly traditional practices affects our essence as opposed to the material world, which never fulfills us. In a traditional religious setting, it is a tribe or group leader who is responsible for our direction. In a nondenominational, nontraditional setting—a modern, New Age approach—we are accountable for our own self-transformation.

Does the term *spirituality* refer to the way people seek and express their life's purpose as they unite in a sacred way? It appears to be a broad concept that emphasizes connection with something greater than ourselves as we wonder why we are here on earth. This search is universal for mankind, one that spans the majority of cultures and individuals.

What is most important is the link between spirituality and love. To connect to your spirituality, you must feel love. Love encompasses feelings of deep affection, fondness, tenderness, warmth and intimacy. It inspires you to crave what is best for another person without considering yourself, a perspective that will result in a feeling of happiness.

Some are generous and lavish with their love. Some are stingy and fearful. And some, unfortunately, are incapable of allowing love to escape from the locked treasure chest within their hearts. Complex feelings are trapped inside until one day they explode, resulting in irrational behavior.

In order to love, we must first practice empathy, compassion, surrender and forgiveness and accept change. We must risk failure, betrayal or rejection. But, as you will discover in my writings, it doesn't matter what others do with their love or think about it. Love is ours to relish and to give, or not. And with that, please accompany me on this adventure to achieve your higher self.

I'll reveal the answers I've uncovered and explore many additional questions. Of course, everyone has their own personal course to follow, as well as their own individual queries and answers, but I started with the questions I've mentioned. My truths may not be yours, but I'll share what I've learned. Finding your purpose is of prime importance. I will discuss why you need that and how to uncover this pure essence that guides your course in life.

Chapter 1
Nature

*Everybody needs beauty as well as bread,
places to play in and pray in
where nature may heal and cheer
and give strength to the body and soul.*

John Muir

ONE DAY, I SAW AN ATTRACTIVE MOTH IN MY FIFTY-DEGREE bedroom that I close off from the rest of the heated house. (This room never warms no matter what I do—I've come to accept that.) The delicate, perky moth, a translucent lime green with blue accents, seemed perfectly content to rest on my white wall. I adored this insect and enjoyed studying him for three days. I watched his stillness; he barely moved. With wisps of wings so perfectly formed, he became my friend. He seemed to exhibit no fear or wish to fly to safer grounds as I leaned down to observe his fragile details.

I wondered, *Should I hit his body, squash him, in case he has a mind to chew holes in my clothes?* He seemed to like hanging out on my wall. He seemed to belong there. So no, I simply couldn't transform him into a flattened blob. Instead, I performed a gentle extraction, releasing him in the garage (a warmer environment than the ten-degree outdoors).

I reflected on what I would have done ten or fifty years ago: crush him for sure so he wouldn't infringe on my realm. Was this a ridiculous fear, like other nonthreatening experiences I encountered in my world of superiority? He could eat my possessions or be a nuisance, but these concerns were no longer relevant to my current reality.

As I develop in my spiritual views, I see minor occurrences like my interaction with this moth as opportunities to shift my daily thinking; each interaction becomes meaningful and magnified as I learn how to treat these treasures of the natural world with respect. Thankful that I didn't annihilate this moth and was able to see the beauty he brought to my world, I allowed him, and other creatures, to live in my imperfect space.

How did I arrive at this benevolent stance? It began with my transformative trip to that mountain, a place that I struggled so hard to reach. My discovery there ignited a new awareness and direction for my life. I became a more spiritual person full of compassion and love.

It's important for you to search for your own brand of spirituality—what moves *your* soul. Nature is my passion, my link to the universe, what makes me tick. Nestled deep within me, it provides an energy source I can use for healing others and myself.

Nature embodies all we are in our world. It is the magic, beauty and strength of its creations that bond me to a spirit beyond myself, a continuum in life. We attempt to uncover nature's mysteries and its connection to us through plants, animals, insects, oceans and sky. When we view this perfection, we are moved to acknowledge that a spiritual power unites this wonder. We feel reverence for the relationship between nature and spirituality. An obligation surfaces to protect each and every thing on earth and beyond. If we are not allied to our earth and its inhabitants, we lose our humanity.

I normally don't talk about this driving force that makes me feel whole and holy because of the reverence it holds for me and others might not understand the depth of what I feel. But from the following stories, you will quickly discern the important connection I have to nature; I must breathe, touch, see and feel it in order to *be*.

My Path Assisted by Nature

Nature amazes me. It nurtures and fills my soul with happiness and peace. It has always affected me in a profound way. When young, I would venture far from our subdivision or to any place without buildings and people in order to connect with a forest, a mountain or an ocean. In these locales, it seemed every fragment in my body relaxed and celebrated.

I see pristine beauty in all natural forms and maybe that's why I've become a photographer. I desire to share this splendor with others.

When we spend time with our environment, we unite with animals and Mother Nature, a restorative experience. The presence of nature is a magnetic pull for me, a connection to past lineages that releases a feeling of tranquility and respect for the many forms of life on our planet. When outside, whether taking a hike in the woods or going on a lunch-hour sidewalk stroll, open your senses to receive sights, sounds, smells and textures. Enjoy the wonders that await you.

I remember relaxing by a riverbed after a long day of driving and setting up camp. I spread my peach-colored towel on the ground so I could lie by a meandering creek outside Hendy Woods State Park near the Mendocino Coast in California. The towel was not long enough for my five-foot-three body so my hands extended over the cotton to rest on the smooth stones.

I've always been fascinated by and drawn to rocks so I studied the unique beauty of each. I closed my eyes, and, in my relaxed state, almost drifted off to sleep when something strange happened. I felt a tingling vibration, maybe a rock's energy, a force I did not understand then.

No, the rocks didn't talk to me out loud, but in feeling those vibrations I acknowledged the unknown. I connected to an inanimate object—weird. We are the product of these natural substances from eons past, forms that date back 3.8 billion years, when meteorites from outer space, often embedded with crystals and minerals, combined with water to form life on our planet. Were my feelings because of our similar cores?

Since that moment I strived to understand my experience by the riverbed and arrived at conclusions mentioned in chapter 7.

Falling Snow, Impending Winter

When the granules indicating winter's first snowfall start to drop from the sky, I am filled with reverence. It's a defining moment, a slice of fall morphing into winter. The flakes signal excitement for what follows—a blanket of white on my mountains and wishes of winter skiing.

The wet snow pelts my windows, a forty-five degree assault, I increase the stove's propane dance during the temperature drop. Now below zero outside, the crystals harden, announcing winter's arrival. In preparation, I have decorated my house, porch and outdoor trees with strands of lights for Christmas. I will not cut down another tree, kill one more this year, or possibly ever, as I retire to my enclosure of warmth inside, a cocoon in which to welcome the coming season, when the rays of the sun are not often seen. I love the snow—skiing and walking down a path in two feet of fluffy white stuff. It will kiss my spirit as I enjoy this winter wonderland and then return home to work on my life passions, light my fire, pour a cab and be joyful.

Blessed, I watch the performance of winter's arrival.

Second Thoughts About the Big Guy

It was my first launch of the 2010 season with my baby orange inflatable kayak. Excitement stirred my body. Projects, travel and commitments had kept me from the water until now. The clear ice melt of Payette Lake enticed my legs to move forward and launch, slide my boat into the water. Soon I was seated at water level. Now one with the liquid and ready to fight swift currents with each paddle dip, I moved ahead.

Why haven't I done this sooner? How could I ignore this pleasure? Memories of past rafting trips on Idaho rivers surfaced, trips where I had survived class IV and V runs; this choppy lake was a piece of cake in comparison. I forged ahead with hard paddle strokes and reached the tranquil north finger of a connecting river.

A soothing calm permeated the early morning, just as I had hoped. Soon the Sea-doos and obnoxious motorboats would be roaring with their loud music on the water—why I had left the lake for this protected wonderland. I dipped my black paddle with intent, trying to perfect each stroke. I soon abandoned thoughts of the past hectic year—I repeated the mantra "Stay in the moment," as I blocked out the annoyances of daily living.

I heard birds calling to each other, squirrels screeching, trying to control their turf, a huge bug splashing at the water's edge and a trout picking up a surprising lunch.

I saw the morning light filtered through pollen. I

smelled the fragrant majestic green firs. I heard leaves rustle. I felt at peace. *Life Is Good!* I thought, feeling pleased with the tranquility I had found.

Then I saw the big guy. He was a huge moose with a full rack, river left. He seemed oblivious to the lady soon to invade his solitary environment; I immediately slowed my strokes but desperately tried to maneuver toward him to get my best shot with my Fuji compact camera. (Yes, I was a professional photographer using a point-and-shoot. Let's not go there with the why.) I needed to be extremely close to this large animal to get a good photo.

I moved closer to the moose, paddle in one hand, tiny camera in the other. I was a bit concerned about tipping over my very underinflated boat. (I try but haven't gotten the knack of a full fill-up.)

A shocker—he spotted me and tolerated my closeness, and then, much to my surprise, I realized his mission. He was trying to reach a peninsula, a short distance from me, perhaps to see a mate or find greener munchies. His immense body gracefully entered the water adjacent to me. I felt remorse that I had never bought the Nikon D90 I'd been saving for.

Breathlessly, I waited in my one-woman craft for him to swim in the river and reach his destination just downriver. When he got out of the water, he shook, like my big lab, and looked at me. I continued with my shoot, respecting his space and acknowledging he would be a dot on photos.

I moved closer, paddling with soft stokes until I was almost at his side. Possibly twenty feet away, I smelled his musk (a scent similar to the breath of my aging dog who needed a dental visit). The moose stood directly in front of me.

His head turned toward me. I was definitely a human

infringing on his turf now. He snorted, which was not reassuring. I was in his world, directly in front of him. Could he possibly be upset with me?

I read his body language (which I had learned from dogs). His ears were now tucked back. *Oh, I get it. This could be dangerous. Okay big guy. I'll stop the photography and give you space.*

Luckily I survived that lesson—*never get close to a moose.* They move swiftly and can kill a person with one slice of a horn. I had no idea, but after recounting my exciting photographic trip on this innocent-looking river to inhabitants of my newly settled home, I learned.

It Was Not in My Plan

That damn tree is attempting to block my view of the mountain. My emotions boiled. *Why is the darn tree there?*

I had this conversation with myself while sitting in my Adirondack chair overlooking my property. The fledgling tree was trying to establish its roots. At first, I reassured myself this defiant emerald sprig would never make it. It would not plant in my life, in front of my perfect mountain view. Soon it would succumb to the dry summer or perhaps the challenges of varmints, including my newly cherished voles. Maybe a fox would pee on its roots. But as I observed it inching toward the sky, four years later, I was no longer sure of my assumption.

What the heck was this defiant shoot doing in front of my greatest view? How dare it grow there? But what could I do? According to the rules of my subdivision, I must not remove trees, so I just kept watching with a wary eye.

The Brundage Mountain is one of my sources of

energy and pleasure, ever since I bought my home years ago. I ski down the mountain and it provides me with daily contentment and vigor. A fledgling tree would not interrupt my meaningful connection with this mountain.

This twig soon grew to adolescence with a solid, straight base. It defied me as it stood directly in front of all I held dear. Each year I viewed the growing pine's presence, saw how it conquered all of nature's challenges. I, however, was determined not to water this thing.

I panicked. Should I go out in the night with the dull blade I had purchased years ago while passing through Medford, Oregon, on the way to the coast? (Nestled in an overgrown backyard, the tool had sat rusting on a decayed wooden bench with a hand-scrolled For Sale sign in front of it. A man, almost appearing as dilapidated as the saw, seemed pleased to put my two dollars in his pocket. We each had a big smile on our faces, sure we had gotten the better deal. *This woman will now have the power to cut*, I had thought.)

One night, as I ate leftover Cordon Bleu I had made the previous evening—a kind of celebration to replace boredom—I sat in the declining light on the patio as sun found its night. I glanced to the north at the power mountain. That twig, my nemesis, had grown and now was a dynamo infiltrating my view.

How dare it defy and conquer me? Yet how gloriously its new juniper lime spouts waved in the wind as a challenging spring storm was building in my face. Truly striking beyond description, this tree was planted for life in this wild land, and in my heart for as long as I existed on my acre parcel of land—*mine*. In that moment, I accepted as I surrendered: nature reproduces as it should, gifting us with the unsuspected.

Animal Spirits

Animals not only play an important role in nature, but they also affect our spiritual practices. If you open your heart, you connect with and learn from them. Shamans and members of indigenous cultures engage with animal guides in their healing work and to understand our universe.

In the past, people acknowledged that humans were one part of our world but also embraced animals in their cultural ceremonies as equals. In recent times, that belief has shifted to raising humankind's status as dominant, distancing us from nature. But if you are willing to embark on a journey to connect with animals, they will richly reward you.

Deer Spirit

Resting on my purple-scribed mat at home, I had just completed my daily yoga, unusually late in the evening. The sun's golden rays barely sliced through the gray, welcoming the still of impending night. For some unknown reason, I was compelled to walk during that beautiful time of sunset along my sparsely inhabited subdivision, toward the trees. (Now practicing living in the moment, I find a deeper joy in seeing spring's vibrant blooms along the paved road during these strolls, even late in the day.)

Through the haze of the mellow rays' last kiss, I rounded a corner, looked up and saw an adolescent doe. She saw me as well. Both of us stopped, wide-eyed, relaxed and interested. Is this possible? Each of us seemed to contemplate the other. At least I did. We studied one another for minutes, staring eye to eye, not risking moving.

Deer spirit

I rejoiced in the pleasure of seeing one of the universe's creatures so close, twenty feet away. Eventually, my irreverence at standing so near to this majestic creature required I divert my eyes.

Initially, I was not sure what caused two dissimilar beings to feel comfortable in each other's presence, so comfortable that neither needed to do anything. Was this trust? We exchanged energy, made a strange connection at sunset. Were we tuned into the same frequency?

Not daring to move one muscle of my body, I wondered could she see me? Was she blind? Why would this animal remain just feet from a human? I unconsciously lowered my eyes, not wanting to be a threat.

Then she moved, not toward the safety of the thick woods but toward *me*. She lowered her head and enjoyed the feast of young fragrant mint sprigs. Occasionally she looked up briefly, studied her surroundings opposite me with more suspicion and then went back to the pleasure of munching spring treats.

In that moment, I saw a wild creature transform into a tame, gentle, trusting animal. Why did she stay so complacently near? When she raised her head, we continued to study each other's posture and faces. But maybe that had no play in the game. Was I witnessing our spiritual connection of safety at close range?

I rejoiced in seeing an animal for this length of time. I concentrated on her damp ebony nose, her enormous inquisitive eyes and her ears twitching like radar.

Finally, five minutes later, apparently tiring of our encounter, she sauntered across the road, barely kissing me by inches. Her charcoal-colored hooves clicked as they struck macadam, all that briefly remained. Once past my still body, she exploded upward toward the diminishing pale salmon sky and landed in a forest of ferns to join her family. It was an encounter I will never forget.

We determine how to communicate in life — with other humans, wildlife, the environment and the universe. All is precious to me and I will remember moments like this with my mind, my senses, and most importantly, my core.

Why Do This?

I packed for one more October venture, acknowledging the challenges as I always did. It was fall, time for my freezing trip to Montana and Wyoming with the usual harsh storms sprouting upon my arrival. I never knew — it could be blissful sunny days or freezing weather, but usually there was snow on this mountain of seven thousand plus feet. Who would have thought that a single woman, seventy-one to be exact, would be up for camping in a tent this time of the year? It is still my passion.

I contemplated this annual trip as I packed; this pleasure was deserved, a time in the mountains I had longed-for all year, a reward as my projects moved to completion. It was my time to experience pleasure in pure, rugged nature.

Never did I factor my safety into the equation just knowing all will be fine.

The decision to go on this trip was confirmed by committing to a cheap hostel in Jackson Hole, Wyoming, that would allow me to attend an annual art event. I would be inspired, take photographs and meet those special souls who were intimately involved in creating this gallery event. It featured the work of artists who inspired my photography, all the years of falling leaves, snow blizzards and soon spring flowers in the fertile soil.

As winter approached, my mind always wandered to the turn of the gentler seasons, spring only a short six months away. I anticipated robins flitting about, deer nibbling my new plantings and gophers digging hollows in the earth. With permission, they ate the only crop I produced—my sweet, ripened red strawberries. We shared. I then confronted the issue at hand, the harshness of this trip.

I would arrive at my campsite to below freezing temperature at night, the fog-laden mornings reluctant to release warmth to the elk who bugle mating calls as they roam the perimeter of my camp.

All of it still amazed me, despite how many times I had endured discomfort camping in the frigid weather to experience the wild.

It was—and still is—a brief time to ignite my soul and be one with the universe. I lingered on my mountaintop before leaving. This trip was different from others that I took to cities. It was a journey into nature, to be among those majestic animals, to immerse myself in the reverence I felt for these mountains, the Sawtooths and the Tetons. This trip renewed me each year. By that point in my life, I had found spirituality. I had learned to live in the *now*. So I happily surrendered to my backpack, gathered my gloves, vortex tops and wool hats.

Why at my age? Because this amazing environment is here for us to record. It's why I ventured to Africa in the early 90s, before their animal population began to disappear. My appreciation of nature only grows. Each trip to this frosty, wild land reconnects me to my essence.

American Indian Spiritual Beliefs About Animal Connections

The oldest type of belief system in the world is animism. It is a conviction that all objects, including creatures, possess a spiritual essence. American Indians accept that animals have souls and a consciousness that exists after death.

I respect the belief systems of American Indians. With over five hundred tribes scattered across the United States, they are bound together through these core principles:

- Never take more than we need.
- Thank the Creator for what we have or what we will receive.
- Use all of what we have.
- Give away what we do not need.

These values allow for infinite interpretations, a *spiritual freedom* that encourages people to live by their personal beliefs rather than the more stringent doctrines organized religions tend to offer.

Many American Indian cultures believe that animals differ from humans through unique attributes only they possess. For example, animals know when and where to migrate; they survive without tools or weapons and appear content in their environment with most living in core families for a lifetime. They do not fight or kill except to establish dominance over their pack and to secure the right to mate. They seem to have affection for each other, which they display with a variety of emotions unless abused by humans. There is no greed, envy or hate. They are able to communicate by touch, smell, body movement, sound and with mental telepathy. It's a common belief among many American Indians tribes that animals live through eternity.

Animals are instinctually aware of human feelings. They tend to sense human fear as well as a broad range of our emotions and personalities. Our expectations create a mood in them as they react.

Many American Indian cultures believe that mystical beings and animal guides choose you and when, or if, to come into your life. A particular guide (pathfinder) must be in harmony with that person. Could that splendid deer I spoke of in my previous story, be my guide?

A pathfinder does not need to be an animal; it could be anything—an angel, an image that speaks to you in dreams, a vibration, a sign, a symbol or words that communicate. It may appear in the form of an ancestor, but regardless the guide speaks to your heart and you need to be open to the idea in order to receive wisdom from your guide. Many American Indians call it "Being one with nature."

Teddy—and Trust

I first met this good-looking, white-colored golden retriever in 2013 when a neighbor brought him to my mountain property. He had an unusual upturned nose; long, soft, silky fur that fell to the earth and big, perfectly formed dark eyes that gazed into your inner soul. One right front paw would not stand erect—it was curved to the left.

None of that mattered. I adored him the second we met.

His long, sad story unfolded. An elderly woman in Washington who was moving to a nursing home wanted to find her doggie a good home. She asked around and found a caring man in her area that committed to help. He soon learned the challenges he had signed up for. The dog, after six years of living with this woman in her apartment and seldom going on walks, wouldn't behave. Teddy longed to jump, run after something he shouldn't, be free after all those years pent up inside. The lady's time came, off to her new subdued life of confinement. The man who had committed to find Teddy a good home began his search for an appropriate place for an animal of this temperament.

My neighbor, Lisa, had heard of this dog's plight. No one else stepped up to take this midlife fellow, so, despite having young children and living miles away, she drove to Washington and loaded this white exuberant retriever into her car. He immediately bonded with Lisa, not her husband who could not get Teddy to do anything for him. Only Lisa.

When she got home, Lisa asked me, "Would you accept this dog that needs a home? He's ninety pounds." (She omitted the fact that he was basically untrained.)

Several years had passed since my lengthy grieving process for Tasha, my cherished dog who died. It might be time for yet one more special animal in my life. Lisa brought Teddy by, unleashed him and drove away. Apprehensive to leave his new home, only two houses away, Teddy longingly gazed after Lisa.

He hesitated, perhaps trying to decide whether to stay. I lowered my body to his level to reassure him. I spoke softly and asked him to look at his new home. Oh no, he would not enter my place after all he had endured—his owner leaving him with a man he did not know and my neighbor newly abandoning him. *Oh No.*

Impatient—I like to make progress—I considered my options and decided I would grab him by the collar and guide him inside. He would adore my home, maybe even smell Tasha. But no way would he move. I dragged this unwilling dog over the hearth into my home as he lay down on all paws. Clearly, he hated this maneuver and surely despised me, but he did not bark, bite or aggressively resist. Teddy remained in a passive position. Political demonstrators could learn from him.

I released my grip and he immediately ran to the door to escape my home, looked longingly for the world beyond, and Lisa. At that moment, I learned something. You can't force any being into loving you or even enjoying your presence. He wanted out, to run to the safely of his home across the plains and never return to this naughty, forceful woman.

Surprisingly, over time, he began coming to my home each day to bark for a biscuit, early in the morning, always a distance from my home. Weary-eyed, I'd rush downstairs in my pajamas, open the frosty door and break up his one treat, congratulating him each time he caught a slice I threw. Once he got what he wanted, he would go on his way, never returning to be petted or sit in my presence. I waited outside with hope, but he'd only show up when he desired a treat.

But soon we began to make progress. One day he stood closer, fifty feet from my property, softly barking—not his usual assertive sound. Each day he moved closer, retrieved his treat that now became two. He didn't know how many he might be able to convince me to give.

Then one day I got the reward instead. He returned at day's end, stood closer than normal to my house, possibly thinking, *what's the worst that can happen?*

I retrieved the treat, sat on the patio, broke it into pieces and presented them to him. He immediately ran up to me and ate all ten pieces out of my hand, drooling all over my clothes! Was this progress after three years? A reward for a woman who wished to control and had learned her lesson? Yup, I would take it.

What does this mean? my analytical, but not dog-centric, mind asked?

After a day when he had not shown in the early morning, in forty-degree temperatures as the sun contemplated leaving, Teddy finally decided to surface. He did not bark but quietly appeared, maybe this time to be near my presence, at least that's what I wished to believe. There was a new connection forming. I was working upstairs yet somehow, in the absence of a bark, I felt his presence and ran down to greet my visitor.

Yes, this majestic guy with his bent front leg, my once potential doggie with a deformity no longer visible in my mind, had captured my love, and after a day's absence, I happily welcomed him. He was here and I no longer worried.

He immediately came up my steps, unusual for him to move so close. He allowed me to pet his head, then his shoulders and body. He nudged my hands and leaned into me, his body begging for more until he lay on my lap, all of him.

We glanced at one another, creating an intimate link. He didn't even want his treat as the wind whipped and his family returned home up the hill.

Eventually, he slowly walked away, our bond secure for some reason, possibly my surrender to trying to fix the past; maybe with patience, we had established a solid connection. Teddy was my sage, the one teaching me.

Chapter 2
Religion and Belief Systems

*When you walk to the edge of all the light you have
and take that first step into the darkness of the unknown,
you must believe that one of two things will happen:
There will be something solid for you to stand upon,
or you will be taught how to fly.*

Patrick Overton

Flow to the universal ocean

We relate to the nonphysical world in many ways; it could be through organized religion or a personal relationship with God, a higher power, art or nature. Often our spiritual relationship is a fluid path, changing throughout our lives.

I grew up attending a congregational church. Erected and then painted white on weekends by its members, the church was an image out of a postcard from the past. Both Mom and Dad volunteered there in various capacities, including teaching Sunday school.

Every seven days, friendly faces from our community surrounded me. We celebrated holidays together as well. I attended summer religious camp on the shores of the gorgeous Saranac Lake. Early morning and late day devotionals overlooked either choppy water or serene lemon-pink reflections that inspired my religious commitment and added to the joy I found in this fellowship.

This communion, in my early teens, moved me to contemplate becoming a missionary. I could save humankind, or maybe a few souls. Since I've connected more directly with my higher spiritual self, I have uncovered the healing aspect of helping others, which is very rewarding. The church instilled in me a moral foundation that remains and fortifies me to this day, but I began examining what spirituality meant in my current life.

I dismissed many church rituals because I could no longer embrace the idea of going to heaven, the threat of hell or—the most difficult concept for me to accept—that I was a sinner. Heck no. Maybe I've made mistakes, but I am extremely moral, living a life of giving and helping others, engaging in acts of kindness. That kind of life doesn't equate with my definition of sin. The church's teaching about the devil also upset me, so I began to reject my years of religious training.

I found myself evolving, leaving behind traditional religious dogma to embrace a nontraditional, nondenominational practice. Like a river, similar to the one in the photograph at the beginning of this chapter, my spirituality is full of twists and turns. It simply moves toward the ocean of the universe, the ebbs and flows advancing through time.

There were moments in my life where I resurfaced under those steeple-topped walls as I raised a family. But ultimately, I stopped going to church because it no longer fulfilled my needs, and many of its doctrines do not align with my current beliefs. I have stayed peripherally connected to the church, but now, I only attend services on holidays. My prior religious practices have become rituals only—no longer my beliefs.

Early in my pursuit of spiritually, I began comparing faiths. I was surprised to find that most organized religions espouse similar basic concepts of love, compassion and morality. Compassion binds a tribe. A positive interaction with a person after a challenging encounter can alter that experience because it buffers, calms and lessens a desire for revenge.

I explored the roots for most organized religions to see if I could find a connection and commonality among them. The human race passed through a totemic stage, a period where people worshipped natural objects or animals, maybe a wolf or bird that a clan adopted as a symbol for strength and unity. Today, most indigenous people in Canada, the United States, Northern New Guinea, Zimbabwe and North India still practice these rituals.

Open to indigenous beliefs, I met two shamans during my world travels. One in the Amazon rainforest introduced me to the healing powers of herbs he grew and used in his practice. He actually healed a bad wound I had received on that trip. The other shaman helped me, in my ill state, to leave Puno, Peru and return to the United States.

Shamans are part-time religious practitioners who act as mediums between the human and mystical world as they heal. They perform their activities when they are fasting or in a trance induced by psychedelic mushrooms or drugs. To communicate with the spiritual realm and access their magic, they may drum, dance, sing, participate in sweat lodge activities, go on a vision quest or ingest plants, such as morning glory, sage and sweet grass.

From these attempts to reach the gods and change the path of others within a clan, organized religions emerged, and, yes, there are similarities in their devotions. I have identified five major religions in the world: Christianity, Islam, Hinduism, Buddhism and folk religion. Christianity evolved from Jewish traditions, and Islam developed from Christianity and Judaism, which both started in the Middle East. Despite their differences, a rich cultural interchange exists between Jews, Christians and Muslims.

World religions have each developed their own dogmas and ceremonies. Religions help define the rules of cultural behavior, dictate the foods we eat, provide celebrations and entertainment and even set the parameters for dating. They impart power and include energy-encompassing rituals that transcend crisis, form a culture's collective wisdom and give meaning to life events such as birth, marriage, adulthood, aging and, finally, death, the passage from one state to the next.

When considering the five major belief systems, Christians represent approximately 32 percent of the world's population. Muslims are 23 percent, Hindus 15 percent, Buddhists 7 percent and followers of folk religion, 6 percent. I've found over forty factions of recognized religions, but there are many more. Most of these groups are included in the Big Religion Chart that is listed among the references for chapter 2. I will briefly outline some of the most popular religions and factions here.

Advaita Vedanta

A Hindu philosophy and religious practice of India, this belief system emerged in the first millennium BCE. It emphasizes knowledge as the path for achieving spiritual liberation. Meditation and a belief that prayer transforms perceptions of our world are most important.

Baha'i Faith

Founded in 1863, this faith has between five to seven million followers who believe that there is one God, the soul is eternal and good and one must develop spiritually to be closer to God. Heaven and hell are states of being. Hard work and education are important. Baha'i believers attempt to influence social justice, live with high moral standards, celebrate equality of the sexes and have a desire to unify the world with peace.

Buddhism

Founded circa 520, Buddhism has about 360 million followers who don't worship a particular God. Buddhism is considered both a religion and a philosophy of living. In their practice, Buddhists seek to avoid suffering, gain enlightenment and work toward a release from the cycle of birth to rebirth. During their life's journey, they attempt to let go of all yearnings. The foundation of Buddhism is mindfulness. Careful attention to body postures and breathing allows the feelings of good, bad and neutral to affect the mind, moods and attitudes while involving all five senses.

Chinese folk religion (Chinese religion)

This indigenous folk religion of China has 394 million followers. This belief system acknowledges yin and yang, mythological beings and folk deities. It advocates for a life of harmony and a belief in reincarnation after death. The government and common people share religious practices and beliefs, which include rituals honoring ancestors, exorcism of harmful forces and a belief in the rational order of nature.

Christianity

Traced to the fourth century BCE, Christianity has approximately two billion followers who believe in the teachings of Jesus and his father, a loving God who answerers all prayers that result in joy. Christian doctrine espouses that all have sinned and salvation is only possible through Christ. Those who accept Christ as their personal savior spend eternity in heaven while those who don't spend eternity in hell. To achieve salvation, prayer and Bible study are necessary. Supporting others, seeking truth and celebrating numerous holidays are important parts of Christianity. Jesus takes a personal interest in the fate of each soul, but the mind determines the quality of an individual's life.

Hinduism

This indigenous religion started to develop between 500 BCE and 300 CE mostly in Nepal and India. Hinduism has approximately nine hundred million followers who believe in one supreme reality (Brahman) who provides all bliss and is the creator and destroyer of the world. Through the cycle of reincarnation, believers work on karmic issues. They seek enlightenment through the practices of yoga, meditation and living one's dharma (purpose/role). Once enlightenment is attained, Hindus are liberated from the rebirth cycle. They believe their actions create their destiny.

Islam

Founded in 622 CE and based on the teachings of Muhammad, Islam has 1.3 billion worshipers. They must submit to God to gain access to paradise after death. Sacrificing their life is one way to achieve this. A belief in paradise or hell, faith, prayers, alms, pilgrimages, and fasting during holidays of celebration are important parts of Islam.

Jehovah's Witnesses

This Christian sect was founded 1878. It has eight million followers who believe in one God, Jehovah. Salvation is achieved through faith in Christ and obeying the laws of this religion. Jehovah's Witnesses see the end of the world as imminent. Heaven is for the fourteen thousand chosen followers while eternity is here on the new earth and for those believers who do not achieve heaven and remain on earth. Nonbelievers will die. There is no hell.

Mormonism

Joseph Smith organized this religion in 1830, which has 12.2 million members. Believing in God the father and Jesus, the son of Christ, Mormons believe in a return to good through acts of kindness, fairness and love. Their practices are further defined by faith, decent work, ordinances and evangelism. They believe some return to the terrestrial kingdom for instruction and to be with God upon resurrection. Some are rewarded but may not be with God; hell is for those that reject God at death. Mormons follow the Christian Bible, Book of Mormon and other doctrines.

New Age

Founded in the nineteenth century, this movement has five million followers committed to this belief: the divine is an impersonal life force, focused on heightened consciousness and world peace through spiritual transformation. Evil comes from ignorance. Followers of the New Age movement believe in reincarnation but also have an interest in astrology, mysticism, crystals, yoga, tarot readings, holistic medicine, psychic abilities, angel communications and channeling. These people believe we are God, he is in us and each person is a complete sovereign over their own life, which creates their individual reality.

Seventh-day Adventist

Founded in 1863, Seventh-day Adventism has approximately twenty-five million followers. They worship a Christian God, and they live by the Bible, concentrating on the Old Testament. Their belief is that a second coming of God will be soon, but followers are now living in the "peace pause" before the resurrection. Then they will reside for eternity in heaven; there is no hell.

Spiritualism

This Christian worldview began in 1850 and has eleven million believers. Spiritualism focuses on death, when the body and spirit become separate. Of prime importance is morality, contact with the divine after life, spirit healing and communication with the departed; guides assist believers in their lives.

Unification Church

Founded in 1954 by Sun Myung Moon, the Unification Church has one to three million followers. It is a monotheistic religious practice with a belief in the duality of God (male and female). It advocates for true affection, world peace instead of selfishness and eternal life in the divine world. Blessing ceremonies are an important part of the practice.

Unitarian Universalism

Formed in 1961, the Unitarian Church has 800,000 members who seek inspiration and insight from all major religions with a central belief in the nature of God. It encourages spiritual growth through a free, yet responsible, search for truth and meaning. Unitarian Universalism also has a deep regard for inclusive love. Church services draw from a variety of belief systems, from agnosticism, to Judaism, to Buddhism and others.

Zen

This school of Buddhism was organized in China in the sixth century during the Tang dynasty. Influenced by Taoism, Zen beliefs spread to Korea and Japan. Today there are 9.6 million people devoted to this practice. It emphasizes exercising self-control, in part through meditation, and helping others.

There's a lot of diversity among major religious beliefs. For example, Hindus believe in multiple gods and goddesses while Buddhists believe there is no god—instead personal development and contributions to society are emphasized. New Age followers believe each person is god while Muslims have faith in a powerful but unknown god. And then Christians assert that God is loving and approachable.

Yet I found commonalities among these religions. Most espouse a god, a single ultimate creator who interacts with the world. The majority of religions believe that sexual chastity is a virtue, and they practice spiritual discipline through prayer (or meditation) and regimens of fasting. During prayer, believers express what is in their hearts without the polarity of right or wrong, without thought, thus it is true feeling and seeing rather than judging. Most religions embrace the practice that the wicked are punished and the righteous will be rewarded. Of prime importance are acts of kindness that bind humanity together.

While religions have their various dogmas, there are still many additional similarities among them. Most of the following concepts and tenants transcend individual religions:

- God is one. There is often a different name for God in different religions.
- God is ever present—God is everywhere.
- God is light—God is hope which illuminates life.
- God is within us—God is in everything.
- Spiritual knowledge is within everyone's reach—you must only search for it.
- The universal name of God is I Am. This common name found in all religions (what God asked Moses

to call him) refers to being kind, creating happiness through love.
- Compassion and respect for self and others are paramount.
- Believers must demonstrate morals—don't lie, steal or commit adultery.
- All humanity is united. Most religions advocate against differentiating between people based on caste, creed, color or nationality. All God's children are embraced as one integrated family.
- Peace and nonviolence are important—religions encourage peacemaking, drawing people, communities and nations into friendship. Most religions suggest overcoming anger to live in harmony.

Once, I asked a Christian a question that plagues many people: "Why is there so much evil in our world, and if there is a God, why does he allow this?"

She said, "Because God gave us free will. Because sometimes horrible things happen for a greater or future good. God is something we do not fully understand because he is not a person and sometimes that is difficult to wrap our minds around; we are only human and that is how we think. We do not know God's overall plan."

Here's another answer according to Josh McDowell Ministry: "The scriptures make it plain that God did not create the world in the state which it is now, but evil came as a result of the selfishness of man. The Bible says that God is a God of love and he desired to create a person and eventually a race that would care deeply for him. But genuine devotion is nonexistent unless freely given through unrestricted choice to accept God or reject him."

Many people establish and explore their spiritual world through organized religion, attending a place of worship to honor their beliefs and to practice rituals in relationship with God. Organized religion can bring a sense of purpose and commonality while providing the power to fulfill personal needs. These followers move along a path dictated by their supreme power; they will be punished if they do not comply. Often, fear is the method through which God reveals truths, and each religion espouses theirs is the only true one.

Yet I can't ignore the fact that many religious conflicts have led to the annihilation of cultural populations, causing death, suffering and extreme unrest. If the human race wishes to prevail, we need to concentrate on the similarities between our beliefs and create unity as we work toward peace.

I tried attending nondenominational places of worship like the Unitarian Church, but that wasn't quite right for me either. Then I began developing my core principles. I contemplated death—my own as well as that of others no longer here on earth. I considered what kind of legacy I would leave behind once I wasn't a worldly person. More importantly, I explored forgiveness and the depths of compassion I had barely considered or understood in the past. I became concerned for humankind, about the demolition of the earth that results from pollution and wars—why does our human race often destroy? How can destruction be replaced with benevolence?

Through the years and after much self-reflection, I found my own brand of spirituality—a higher spirit that I could cleave to that would support and guide me in life. I have moved from a traditional Congregational faith to a more flexible belief system that continues to evolve. It has been a very personal exploration. I share this journey with you in the hopes it will guide your own search.

I believe in the interconnected nature of the universe, meditation as a path for enlightenment and the importance of giving to others. These core beliefs feel right for me so I have stopped looking, though I continue to grow by seeking ways to better live these beliefs each day. They suit me. I navigate my road to enlightenment by taking responsibility for my actions, finding solutions through thought and discoveries, and engaging in acts of love. On this spiritual journey, I have found the courage to confront and dissipate fear.

A 2016 article titled "It's Hard to Go to Church" that appeared in the *Atlantic* stated that although 40 percent of people believe in God and pray at least once a week, they do not identify with any particular faith. A *Newsweek/*Beliefnet.com poll states that 79 percent of the religious pray once a week, but only 45 percent attend worship services, suggesting that many people are searching for a different way to define and communicate with their spiritual world.

In 1999, Beliefnet.com suggested that our nation was in the middle of a metaphysical boom. Movies and television shows like *Angels*, *Touched by an Angel*, and *Dominion* attest to this transformation. There has and continues to be a shift from following organized religion to seeking nontraditional spiritual beliefs.

Baby boomers are specially shopping for faith. One reason is the need to feel purpose in their lives. In past generations, conflicts served to bind us as a society—World War I and II, Vietnam and Watergate. The *fear* resulting from recent events has created emptiness and a loss of security. Faith institutions are no longer meeting the needs of many baby boomers. A 2015 Pew Research survey uncovers similar results, indicating that baby boomers are less likely to practice their religion in church. They are practicing in a new way, leaving traditional places of worship as they experiment with alternative paths to reach their higher power.

According to Religion News Service, participation in organized religion has declined twice as much over the past fifteen years (up to 2013) as it did in the 1960s and 70s. Millennials, in particular, have increasingly dropped out of organized religions. The Pew International Project states that 64 percent of Internet users searched for spiritual information on the web. It seems people are no longer relying on past places of worship to fill their souls.

I probably fit the mold of the baby-boomer generation. Though I dismissed my traditional religious beliefs when I became disenchanted as an adult, my childhood experiences in the church set me on the path to discover a higher power in nature as my place of worship.

Today worshipers recognize they can create their own religious smorgasbord by picking and choosing components that have particular meaning to them, discarding some as they continue to pile food high on their plate of new spiritual discoveries. We are now into self-help and open to new ideas, no longer tethered to traditional loyalties.

Brand allegiance diminished or dissolved with this baby boomer generation. Some assume that if organized religion doesn't have a practical application they simply won't participate. They no longer see the value of honesty, authenticity and prosperity. Past efforts of striving for material goods and financial stability don't seem to be working as they suffer in crisis, lacking joy. Armed with knowledge about self-actualization, they often don't contemplate or act.

A majority of people no longer believe that institutional religion's strict doctrines are in control of their spiritual lives—*they* are. In their search for spiritual connection they are now more metaphysical as they gain an enhanced awareness of who they are. They are growing in harmony with their inner selves, confronting existential dilemmas.

Twenty-year olds tend to feel immortal as they explore and experiment. In their thirties, people often search for a soul mate and a greater sense of purpose. They may busy themselves with creating families. As we continue to age, we are faced with our mortality, often watching those closest to us die. We must also find strength to care for our parents, our kids and ourselves, perhaps longing to connect to others and the world in a more profound way. As we age, we tend to intensify our spiritual search.

Where are you in your spiritual journey, uncovering what you wish for in life and the hereafter?

40 Days of Peace– Creating Community and World Change Through a Relationship with God

I had the pleasure of meeting Kit Cummings during a visit to the Pomerado Region of the San Diego Church of Christ in California. We talked about my interest in world peace and how his wonderful, worldwide efforts contribute to that vision through God and love. This is a story of one man changing the lives of difficult-to-reach criminals through compassion and his relationship with God.

Kit is the founder of the Power of Peace Project (POPP). Through POPP, he works with people incarcerated in maximum security prisons within the United States to instill peace among the offenders in these institutions. Following the success of the 40 Days of Peace program, his initiative spread to other prisons around the world. He also established a program to help steer troubled youth toward positive life goals, away from drugs and criminal activity. He achieves these objectives by forming relationships between churches and communities.

His motto is Hope is the New Dope. It works. He communicates with the converts in a way only he is able to. The first time I met Kit, I was startled by his arms. They were covered in thick black tattoos. Then I glanced up, way up, to see that his beard had hints of steel gray. He was probably not your ordinary church attendee. But he was personable and open to my invasion of his territory after a church service. We discussed our missions and our hope for peace.

He told me he was preparing for a community service project, escorting some drug addicts to Guatemala where they would build schools. He wanted to expose his volunteers to another culture and high poverty areas with the hope that it would be a life-changing experience, encouraging them to work on their drug problem. He wanted these kids to get high on life and feel the joy of service, but his most potent message was about experiencing a world of love.

The POPP mission is designed to work with the new generation, many of whom are armed with technology, and often little else. Many children of this generation have no real life purpose driving them. The evolutionary changes of technology has left many young people in limbo, void of emotion except when acting out or interacting with a computer screen.

Something is missing . . . a cause. Many of this generation want to skip all the valuable steps learned by their parents and move directly to "GO" to win a prize. Kit teaches them not to run from pain but embrace it and to replace fear with courage. He connects intimately with these troubled kids, finds commonality and encourages them to make amends when wrong. He motivates them by dangling their family's welfare and bond in front of them—"Reform so your children don't follow your example." It works. He exudes inspiration, commitment, and underlying it all is his depth of caring.

Many wonder how Kit could bring these hardened criminals to sign a document promising they will peacefully resolve their incarceration challenges over the next forty days—and then actually follow through. This contract encourages them to find common ground with their adversaries by actively listening to what they have to say—and pausing—before answering. This approach represents compassionate communication—treating everyone with dignity and respect and using one's influence for peace. It doesn't end there, however. The tough stuff must be done; when wrong, the inmates promptly admit it and make amends.

The inmates Kit works with hear these powerful messages: You become what you see. You find what you look for. My words create my world. I find what I believe I deserve. What I focus on expands. What I resist persists. All I need I already possess.

These men practice a lifestyle of nonviolence for forty days. Others notice and become curious; after all, it is unusual for someone not to prefer harmony and compassion in their sterile environment. The men find that they are not labeled as weak, as they fear, but rather they are respected. It spreads through institutions.

Life is what made Kit relate to these troubled men and boys. A preacher for twenty-five years, he turned to drugs when he became disillusioned with life. He searched and found his mission to help others and find peace. Now he works with organizations such as the National Community Faith Leadership Initiative and Oprah Winfrey's Belief Team. He has also spoken at the Gandhi Global Peace Summit and is a frequent speaker at corporate events. He has written numerous inspirational books and has traveled the world with his mission.

Kit's vocabulary is peppered with the word *God*, and he practices many of the core principles common to most religions with an emphasis on caring for and empowering the lost generation. The people who come into Kit's life become family. In fact this church where I met him is one enormous family offering unconditional friendship.

Kit's Power of Peace Project spans cultures and socio-economic status. His message is one of unlimited power and potential, how the search for God in unusual places—prisons, juvenile detention centers and schools—can create meaningful global relationships.

As we navigate our technology-filled, hyperconnected, diverse world, we collide with and judge those who are different from us. If we approach others with compassion and fairness, might we find common ground?

Chapter 3
Angels Among Us

*We are each of us angels with only one wing,
and we can only fly by embracing one another.*

Attributed to Luciano De Crescenzo

Angels by Our Side

ANGELS AND SPIRIT GUIDES ARE BY YOUR SIDE, WHENEVER you want to receive them. They are sweetness, and here to assist us. How do I know? Keep reading the parables I've included in this chapter that have convinced me. Guides might be earthly persons that are one level above a normal mortal. They may be a relative or friend who has passed. We all have a guardian angel who is here at our birth and remains until our death. Their mission is to give advice, comfort, warning and protection but not to interfere with free will or make decisions. You will feel relaxed in their presence.

Then there are the unearthly universal forms, angels who have never walked on earth. They respond to our requests for guidance and protection and are on call all the time. They help especially when our intent is to bring happiness and healing to the world. It brings them joy to assist. For me, they do not have a religious orientation but they may for others. I would define them as having grace from the ethereal world. I have two angels that look similar to my picture in chapter 4, "Death and Living with Purpose."

From what I've learned, angels can take any shape. They may be visible or not, and they could even be an animal or an inanimate object. Angels have an electromagnetic field around them and vibrate at high frequency.

I've been told that people can have anywhere from eight to over thirty angels watching out for them—so what's up with my meager two? Well, they seem to do the trick, keeping me out of trouble and comforting me when I need to make difficult decisions or request assistance for others. Who knows what exists in our sphere? I find it reassuring and wonderful to have my two angels in my life. And finally, for me, their pure force never tells but *shows*, helping me to uncover direction when requested.

If you invite and welcome angels and guides into your world, they will bless your life as well as the lives of others. Whether you acknowledge them or not, they stand silently by your side, waiting for an invitation.

One way to give angels permission to enter your life is to sit in a peaceful, meditative state and ask them to come. As I go deeper in my spirituality practices, I focus on connecting with people in need; I have started asking my angels for specific ways to heal or to help others during my daily meditation. The results are astounding, and I have included some of these stories in this book as well as my book *Survival Quest*. Along with their guidance in assisting others, I receive serenity and joy when they are in my presence.

The existence of angels in my life makes me feel honored, safe and amazed. I hope you have the same pleasure. After all, welcoming them into your life is simply about true essence—theirs and what you uncover within yourself, sometimes early in life, sometimes later. The following story is about my granddaughter's special gift.

Angel in Training

This angel was born in 2005 and since then has been an integral part of my life for twelve years. The first time I met her she was six months old. My daughter carried this babe in a sling. Her chubby pink cheeks greeted me as I bent down to grin at her. I couldn't believe this lovely girl. Her blue eyes looked at me, this gushing stranger.

"Ava, this is your Grandma!" I had driven over one thousand miles to greet her, a meeting that thrilled me.

This miraculous baby was my daughter's second child. Determined to create a sibling for her first, she had struggled through preeclampsia for a second time. Shaking inside with excitement and wonder, I now met my second grandgirl—another glory enlarging our family circle. She gurgled, explored my face as I returned her gaze with a smile of pleasure. At that moment, we connected.

It wasn't long before I discovered what linked us, the energy, our spiritual joining, similar to what I had noticed with my daughter and did not understand when she was young; I surrendered to this little soul of a new generation. I would never tell anyone, until now, about our connection.

My daughter, Nicole, possesses this special ability to understand people and their essence. It was something she developed during her teen years, possibly earlier. She has a unique intuitive perception of present and future events in others' lives, whether she is currently with them or not. It's a powerful gift.

When Nicole was young, I would ask myself about this force I did not understand. Eventually I accepted it and stopped questioning my daughter's additional senses—sixth (her intuition, her cosmic sense of herself and others) and seventh (telepathy).

I now understand Nicole's gift to be a life spirit. She is a more vibrant spiritual person than normal mortals. My daughter's needs seem to get miraculously fulfilled; she's always able to find a space in the crowded parking lot of life. She experiences premonitions and exudes a calm sense of assurance that allow her to move through life with compassion. My granddaughter Ava seems to have this same ability too.

I saw their actions but did not know the why. But, during my exploration on spirituality, it became clear.

When Ava was a young child, unaware of her "gift," I observed the empathy she felt for others, her penchant to help, her caring and energy, how she'd say the right thing at the right time to enlarge another person.

She'd say funny statements: "I am a celebration," and "My manager is calling me," referring to her mom. Then as she developed, I could see her moving further along her special path. She'd leave notes for her mom: *I believe in you. You will do amazing things today! Never doubt yourself! Be confident. Love, Ava.* This is from a child who is on the spiritual path.

When she was ten, she became even more supportive. I was concerned about some extensive facial surgery I was about to undergo, but I never expressed my fears to anyone. How horrid would I look for the rest of my life?

Prior to the operation, Ava took my hand in hers, delving deep into my eyes and spirit. She said, "Grandma, you will always be beautiful to me—both inside and out." That went a long way in propping me up. I knew it was true and if others couldn't see my beauty, it did not matter.

In my life, I have never enjoyed such closeness with anyone else as I have with this child. With her lavish affection and compassion, sometimes I didn't know how to react to the benevolence of good that flows from her, but I struggle to accept it.

I visit my family often, two states south. Once, when the time came to return home to my world, a farewell changed my perspective on life—the leaving and the giving.

Ava held me close, not too tight but with a passion unusual for a ten-year-old child. She was sharing her total self with me in that long, four-minute good-bye hug. She kept holding me. Who hugs for that length of time?

At first, I was overwhelmed at our closeness; it felt too long to be connected to a person. But then I considered that she needed this extended good-bye before I closed the door. I surrendered to the moment of pure caring. It was an amazing moment of sharing for me, and one I will never forget. The hug was such a simple act, yet her deep affection and joy transferred to my soul with a desire to never let her go. I will carry that closeness, that long embrace, with me forever.

Angel Child of the Wreck—It Certainly Was Not My Fault

When I arrived at my daughter's home in San Diego, it was a fine day. I unpacked. We got reacquainted, exchanging stories about what had been going on in our lives, and sprinkled in hugs and kisses. It was a period of bliss to once again share each other's souls and connect as a close family of joining.

Prior to visiting my daughter's family, I injured my back by lifting heavy stepping-stones to construct a walkway and planting a tree. I then embarked on a three-day drive to camp and see the girls, which did me in. Enclosed in my tent, sweating in 107-degree temperatures, harassed by mosquitoes and yellow jackets, I surfaced with a herniated disk and muscle spasms of angry rebellion. While I knew I should learn to avoid actions that extended beyond my body's limitations, I remained ever defiant.

The day after I arrived at my daughter's house, I woke to debilitating pain, but I refused to submit to it. What right did pain have to inflict havoc on my life, disrupt precious time with my family and our upcoming plans to visit the East?

My daughter mentioned the word I abhor—*doctor*. I told her no. I would recover on my own, hopefully sooner rather than later.

Despite my horrific pain, I needed to go on one short drive to a grocery store five miles away. I adore the treats of Trader Joe's, and I don't have one in my hometown. Looking back, my choice to drive there was about fulfilling a want, probably not a need, but off I went anyway.

This store is a San Diego success story. Young, affluent high-tech earners stock up on the weekend, wanting the best international foods at a fair price. It's their place. When I arrived, the parking lot proved a challenge: every single narrow parking space was full. The lot was almost impossible to navigate with all the bulky, mostly shiny, new black SUVs (which one must drive here for a number of reasons).

As I glanced into that black sea with no open spots, my back screamed to be done with all this. I contemplated the new generation of techies, identified by their T-shirts and bumper stickers. They seemed to think nothing of going on a spending spree to possess the latest gadgets. The bike racks and extensions hanging from their cars seemed to indicate a readiness to excel at any sport. They rushed from place to place, cell phone in hand, never still, although they worked for companies that espoused a newer, greener world of peace.

For a simple Idahoan girl, it was difficult to fathom—this obnoxious display of lifestyle. After all, I still packed a four-by-six REI tent, hiked in the woods and paddled an inflatable kayak stored in a fairly compact bag always in my trunk. No ostentation there, just pleasure and serenity.

After doing three frustrating loops of the lot, I spotted someone vacating a spot. While the driver backed out, I contemplated my long to-do list. Now I see that I became one with the masses in their mission to attack, slash and conquer the shelves of this store—I'd grab pita chips, humus and, best of all, Trader Joe's "Two-Buck Chuck" (an acceptable every day wine at $2.99 a bottle).

My blood pressure accelerated. I needed to be the first to grab this sliver of a parking space. It would require a sharp right and then an abrupt forty-five degree turn. I could pull it off, if I was careful. But I was not careful. To claim that spot, I was competing against other drivers who had acquired more training than I had on their daily jaunts around the city. But I was confident I would succeed; after all, I had spotted the space first.

The other drivers didn't back down. I stepped on the gas, made the turns and would soon be headed to my safe harbor—a trip into air-conditioning, an escape from the ninety-degree plus temperature outside. I could see an end in sight; I would be out of this store soon with all my essential goodies and headed back to my daughters. I'd skip the rest of my list.

Nope.

I heard a crunch, which is never a good sign when driving your car in a crowded California parking lot. I stopped immediately. My stomach constricted, all tangled inside. Somehow I had hit a big black shiny car next to me. How could I have thought I could make that turn? Because I was hot, in pain, fatigued and in a rush.

I couldn't believe it. I was always so careful, yet I definitely heard the sound of crunching metal. I visualized the damage inflicted on that car. I imagined the probably very successful owners and their infuriation with the desecration of their pristine, very expensive vehicle.

My world stopped at that moment. Talk about living in the *now*. I got it, focused only on what was unfolding. I decided to back out of the spot, assess the damage, acknowledge the damage and accept the painful consequences.

Another loud *crunch*. I had wedged my car against that big black beast. My attempts to inch backward or forward were futile. Surely, this would cost lots of $$s. I put the car in park, jumped out to access the destruction I had caused.

Nothing, no marks.

Then, in horror, I looked at my car, a surreal sight. Somehow, a silver appendage on this black thing had stabbed my car in the wheel well, plunging into the gray space above my tire, impaling my unfortunate Xterra twelve inches deep.

Oh, my Xterra, my humble unsuspecting gray knight in armor had been injured. The assailant was a huge metal bike rack, with no bike attached. Its name, Thule, glared in a defiant position extending beyond the car's width. Did they not slide it back into position after use or did my car trigger its trajectory?

I wanted to be someone else, to be somewhere else, back or forward in time so I could erase this incident. But of course I couldn't. And the owner(s) of the car were nowhere in sight.

As they say, I never saw it coming—this low beast of a bike rack had been waiting to damage my car. My driver's seat sits high; this interloper sat below the trunk of their car and was not visible during my dance of turns. I thought I had cleared their rear bumper, but this metal thing had attacked my car. There would be no uncoupling of our two vehicles without an act of God or heavenly angels.

All that churned in my mind were dollars—funds reserved for our trip to Walt Disney World that would now be drained by this mishap.

Still standing outside my car, I attempted to release the offender and it simply would not budge in any direction. It remained stuck in the bowels of my car, the two appearing to be in a bizarre mating ritual. *Oh, I must be losing it*, I thought. Each possible solution I came up with was more ridiculous than the last (a side-by-side towing of these joined cars).

Sweat dripped from my body. When I left Idaho, the temperature had been in the sixties. This felt like the tropics by comparison. My herniated disk didn't approve of my stress or standing on my feet. My pain was approaching a nine out of ten. I did what I seldom do for myself, only others; I silently implored my angels for assistance.

Within seconds, two darling girls and a handsome lad, all in their early twenties, rushed to my side. One of them asked, "What can we do to help?" Why had they arrived to help at that precise moment?

They proceeded to wiggle the bent rack frame. Then one girl, studying to be a mechanic, borrowed a tool from a bike shop to remove the bolts. They guided me to drive a fraction of an inch forward, then back, repeating this motion until, finally, we decoupled the cars.

I searched the brown eyes of the mechanic-in-training who had figured out how to disconnect our two vehicles and said, "You are angels." She appeared puzzled. I then explained the subject of my new book and gave her my business card. She smiled warmly and ran off to Trader Joe's to gather provisions for the beach party they had planned on going to over an hour ago, if there hadn't been an act of fate. She probably didn't get it, but I did.

They were calm, kind and knowledgeable — this trio was exactly what I had needed in my harried state. I had experienced an unpretentious act to help a fellow human, just doing what is right. Maybe an angel is not some godly aberration but an everyday flesh-and-blood person who cares.

Surprisingly, upon returning home and reporting the accident, I received the following e-mail:

Hi Sally,

I just wanted to say that you seemed so sweet and nice when me and my friends were helping with your car! My name is Brianna, and before I helped you I really didn't believe in angels, but now, after you told me about your books and about your personal belief in angels, as well as how we were three angels that came to help you, I do. Thank you so much for opening my eyes to the world of angels, fate and good karma! I hope you have a wonderful rest of your day, and that you get all the help you need whenever you need it!

Maybe if we were all kind, more loving, could we change the world together?

Spiritual Support, Angels Working to Help My Friend

It works—sending energy to support and aid someone you care for.

Addy is my hairdresser. How much feeling and caring is involved in that relationship? Ask any woman—loads. Through the years we have yakked about her family and my family, her adventures and my adventures and our belief systems.

We started out having simple conversations that became more complex over time as our affection for each other grew, our hair appointments becoming an excuse for sharing with each other. Even though there were years between us, probably thirty, somehow we connected and enjoyed our two-hour sessions.

She introduced me to health-food recipes while I was transitioning to a more vegetarian diet, and I told her about my romantic misadventures. We discussed our children's challenges and delights, how we could find new ways to work out and continue our self-improvement paths.

Then there was that day. The hair salon called to cancel my appointment with Addy. When I asked why, I heard the answer you never want disclosed. "She's going in for breast surgery next week."

Numb, I couldn't believe this effervescent, fit and spiritual lady could be encountering such a challenge in her young life. Selfishly, I contemplated losing someone who should not be so close to me, given our relationship was based on hair-coloring appointments every six weeks. Yet she was.

I rejected the whole idea. No, she'd be fine. Did they make a mistake with the biopsy? Absorbed with her diagnosis, I sat at my kitchen counter. I raged for a bit, told myself it's not fair, played with denial.

Then I came to acceptance. I would not let her go through this alone. I would be with her every step, every morning during my meditative practice.

Each daily session, I included her in my mantra, asked my angels to assist her. Our support team, just me and my angels, would be there to help fight that nasty cancer, but knowing how spiritual she was—I knew she unconsciously allowed me to send my angels to her side, put their wings around her and help relieve her pain—most importantly, she allowed them to guide her in the fight for her life.

During my meditations, I would see those precious angels sit by her, helping her emotionally navigate the darkness, helping her find a new path toward light.

One day, concentrating on writing my book and achieving my goal for the week, I needed to assess how I would spend each hour away from this pursuit. People and occurrences in the outside world can be distracting, but there were frequent surprises, opportunities and events that are meant to affect your path if you are present and accepting. It's like fate waiting to influence your life, but you need to be out of your normal environment to receive. So this day I contemplated taking a break from my loft perch to write at my local coffee shop instead. It could be therapeutic and productive, but then I often saw friends who would interrupt my focus. No, compelled for some reason, I decided to go.

Something aligned in the universe that day because Addy, accompanied by visiting relatives, was standing in line for food at the coffee shop. She'd had her surgery. She was moving, talking, so much like her normal self—with an edge of submission but a will to conquer.

Her long locks had been cut into a very short style. I didn't know what to call that stylish sweep to one side. When we spoke, she said all her hair was falling out from chemo so she might as well have a good style before all was lost.

She glowed as I hugged her. She talked about how her life had changed for the positive with this new challenge—she had found a new, very optimistic direction in life. This encounter, challenging death, had changed her whole perception of living—what is important and where she is going in the future.

She was an avid reader and in the two short months since I had seen her and she had received the diagnosis, she had explored all she could about her condition and then moved forward into spiritual exploration. Her life had inverted. Energized, she would soon surface in a new profession as a yoga teacher.

My heart was full, full of hope for Addy and her family, with much gratitude for those hard-working angels of mine. They never disappoint when I ask for their assistance. What the heck should I do to show my appreciation for all their devotional acts to save those I care about? Do you think they would enjoy homemade brownies?

A big shout-out for angels !!!!!!!

Chapter 4
Death and Living with Purpose

*I'm not afraid of death because I don't believe in it.
It's just getting out of one car and into another.*

John Lennon

When I was younger, I refused death—for myself, my family, for close relatives and even friends that died. I would not recognize or acknowledge the pain of an adored one's end. Never able to see or embrace them again was unthinkable. It was not in my vocabulary of possibilities.

However, that didn't stop death. I tried, but there it remained, so I buried it.

I grew in many ways through experiencing the painful death of my friend Michael. Finally, I accepted death; I even learned to celebrate his relief from the pain of daily living and the nirvana he was now enjoying, in my own way. I forgave him; I embraced his life and the gifts he gave me.

Something miraculous happened to assist in this shift. Michael supported me from another dimension. When I was newly grieving his loss, he would sit on my bed and talk with me, comfort *me* in the night. At first I experienced jubilation, believing the unbelievable—he had not passed. He was still here with me. But upon opening my eyes, I soon realized that was not quite true. He no longer belonged in my sphere; I suffered with sadness and longed for a different outcome for him—my best bud. How could I go on? Who would I discuss the mundane with? Who would give me guidance?

During his subsequent visits, he'd check on my recovery, listen to my chatter and then take off again. I did not understand why his body appeared gray now, absent of color. Finally, days later, I accepted he was gone—I was ready to release him.

On a walk through the woods, among high snowdrifts, I said an earthly good-bye. I told Michael he must permanently move *up there*. I told him that I adored him, always would, but that he must go to wherever souls go to find their brand of paradise. I needed to begin my recovery, return to living and loving life.

He obliged. At that moment, a huge squawking crow flew a few feet over my head. That noisy, powerful bird, with such an enormous wingspan, had to be Michael, soaring to the heavens, having the last word.

Occasionally, I see him with another bird, continuously calling to me. They fly in tandem, closely connected by their other world. A new partner, perhaps? The thought brings me contentment.

Michael seldom comes to visit so substantially, as in my bedroom to listen, but I give thanks for all he taught me and share that gratitude each morning in my mediation practice.

It's been three and a half years since his passing, and I sense his presence more intensely at times than others, but the few times I have needed to draw on his strength, he has assisted. Once during a surgical procedure I had been given local anesthesia but was still awake. I was uncomfortable and frightened. I asked for his hand to clutch during the ordeal. I clung tightly to my guide's hand, full of life and warmth, through each cut and stitch, until it was over. I will never forget his compassion and support.

Through that experience, I learned people never completely leave you, if you desire. It is possible for relationships to be unending. I know Michael will always be an important part of my life. He served a purpose in my cycle, to help me understand that valued people in my life wouldn't simply "move on" at death but would remain linked to me forever.

Years later, when I heard my good friend Bob had been diagnosed with Alzheimer's, a disease that eventually would take his mind and body, my grieving was less poignant. My experience with Michael had taught me that our relationships do not have to be severed by death.

I will tell you the powerful story of Bob's battle with Alzheimer's disease and his death, but first I want to talk about living with purpose—living in the Now—so we do not have regrets when the time comes to leave our earthly bodies.

As young people, we seldom acknowledge our mortality; we don't think about it until a current event threatens our existence—like a terrorist acts or the increasing brutality in our cities. Scared, stressed out and irritated, we frequently disconnect. But numbness does not help us cope; instead it abets our escape.

Often when someone is diagnosed with a terminal illness, they began to clearly grasp what matters in life. They, and their family members, may reflect upon meaningless, superficial and unauthentic habits of living, and try to change them. The final days represent a chance to eliminate past negative behaviors and replace them with more positive ones, and often this process is accompanied by immense growth. The dying approach a doorway to another world, which they can reject, ignore or step through, finding enlightenment.

In times of crisis with a terminal diagnosis, the need for family and friends to listen becomes clear. A person can acknowledge the dying person's feelings, help their precious one in practical ways and learn from them. It is an opportunity to acknowledge their own mortality and how to better deal with their future.

Hospice can guide families in these tasks and the spiritual work of dying. The purpose of palliative care, hospice, is to review the dying person's life—note the people who have had an emotional impact, those who were disloyal and those who inflicted wounds; uncover the dreams that never materialized and celebrate events that contributed meaning to their existence. Forgiveness is an important part of this process, which often results in peace. Sometimes the dying even draw comfort from planning their own death ritual.

In addition to providing guidance, hospice listens. Patients talk about feelings—love for their children, spouse and friends. They ponder what they gave unconditionally, what they didn't know how to offer or what was betrayed. If they are blessed, they may talk about what they granted themselves.

The terminally ill learn the beauty of surrendering to the next world. Death does not take the person away, only their body; all the accumulated moments you have shared with that person remain in your memory for a lifetime and possibly beyond. Many cultures honor their past relatives, by making alters to them, which enable these loved ones to live eternally in their lives. Death rituals remind us of our mortality, that our time is limited and we need to do whatever we desire—now.

Wouldn't it be best to live, from this moment forward, a life of no regrets, so you do not need to encounter them near the end of life? We need to do whatever we wish today; there will be an end to the becoming.

An article from *A Place for Mom Senior Living* newsletter,

"Living with Purpose," highlights the five recurring regrets of the dying: not living true to oneself, working too hard, not expressing feelings to others, not staying connected with friends and not allowing oneself to be happy.

Here are some ideas about how to change your life so you don't die with these regrets.

Find the courage to live who you are. Don't focus on pleasing others.

Express your feelings. Genuinely share your emotions with those whom you have developed a deep bond. It may be difficult, but learning how to do this and why is important and will create your authentic self. What do you have to lose in expressing these feelings? There is so much to gain.

Find your life purpose and aim to live it daily. There is no true fulfillment unless you concentrate on your purpose. You may have to work less to achieve this purpose — recognize that the accumulation of money, possessions and prestige seldom provide the inner joy and calm you seek.

I left the work environment at age fifty-five and never regretted that decision. It requires me to live a simple life without a major income, but it allows me to engage in the world I adore — pursuing self-help writing, photography, travel adventures and outdoor sports. These activities fulfill my desires, allow me to just *be* and explore opportunities that present themselves.

Maintain your relationships. This is not easy in our fast-paced lives; it matters more than you imagine — for you and those you care about. You may need to work at it harder than the person you are connecting with, but making the effort to maintain relationships over time is richly rewarding and one of the major reasons people survive physical and emotional crises.

Accept happiness. You deserve it! If you transition to living in the present, not the past or future, you'll find abundance. It is hard for us to do this; we are often consumed by the past, obsessed with unresolved problems or mistakes. Focusing on the past feeds our personality and outlook in a negative way. On the other hand, escaping to the future isn't the answer either. We can't control future outcomes; it creates a life of fear and anxiety that is uncomfortable.

Spiritual work requires changes to lifelong patterns. For me, this work uncovers serenity and joy. It allows me to live with true zest so I can savor each day, each hour, each moment—living in the Now. That's where I live more and more, with a bit of effort to redirect at times when I regress. As I grow, it becomes easier and I enjoy more time in this place. Happiness emerges.

The Bravest Thing I've Done

Braveness comes in many forms. Sometimes it's a bold, defiant act where you confront fear head-on. But sometimes bravery is subtler. Sometimes it means doing the right thing out of love, even when others don't see it.

Perhaps the act of bravery I am most proud of is how I chose to say good-bye to my aging dog—straight on, not allowing someone else to do the hard ending. This is due to the devotion and fondness of our bond.

My greatest companion for thirteen years, Tasha accompanied me though the best and the worst times of that period of my life. A rescue dog, Tasha was a three-month-old Lab-Rottweiler mix (and who knows what other lineages). Her story and her actions made a definite

Tasha, my best doggie (don't tell my other ones)

impact on me. Tasha's mother had been wandering the streets pregnant when a kind woman discovered her plight and made a comfortable place for her where she birthed Tasha and twelve other puppies.

Dogs have come into my life at various times. When my family or I simply wanted to share our lives with an animal, we'd usually adopt one from the American Society for the Prevention of Cruelty to Animals (ASPCA).

This time was different. My friend Ed knew of my longing to have just one more dog, so he kept encouraging an event that would create that union. Sometimes he would hear of a friend of a friend who knew someone who knew of a dog just waiting for a home. He combed websites and the newspaper for an opportunity. He understood I wanted a pup that would grow into a large companion for me. I followed up on all the opportunities

Ed presented, but none of them panned out. I got discouraged. I was afraid that I would never connect to my special one, so I resigned myself to being dogless.

Then the universe, knowing what would be right for me and for that animal, intervened. It seemed to push Ed to make one last call, and he encouraged me to go to a mall where a rescue center had some pups I could check out. A waste of time, surely, but I made one final attempt. Positive there would not be a puppy available, I looked at all the middle-aged tails wagging. Turning to leave, something stopped me and pushed me toward the woman who was orchestrating this adoption event. It was unusual for me to approach someone with a request, but I asked her if she had any puppies.

Warmly smiling, she pointed toward a box. There was only one puppy with straight hair, and she was harassing her sleeping brothers and sisters, poised on top of them and nipping each one, perhaps hoping they would romp with her. I just gawked. When the lady asked if I'd like to hold any for a bit to see how it felt, I wanted to run. I had been searching for over a year, but I realized I hadn't prepared to bring one home. Besides how could I chose?

But I didn't have to because Tasha chose me. She was the alpha pup. Unsuccessful in finding a playmate among her siblings, she looked in my direction, her tail wildly wagging. Then she ran to the side of the box nearest to where I stood and tried to leap into my arms. That was the defining moment.

A forceful connection surfaced between me and this wild lady who curled up on my lap when we got in the car. Not expecting to adopt a dog that day, I had no crate or provisions to welcome her, but we drove home together anyway. I couldn't let her go.

She had a definite effect on my life from the start. I launched into craziness, reducing my hours to part time so I could stay home with Tasha. I declined social engagements to hurry home to be with her after my workday. I rejected the fanatical technical reading required to "get ahead" in my position. I even stopped all my shopping expeditions, which used to seem so important, just to spend time with her. I discovered an unplanned sense of balance in my life that I had not pursued in the past.

But my old goal persona surfaced with a vengeance as I delved into insane pursuits. I bought a beat-up Mazda '84 truck. I hated trucks because they symbolized the working class. Bashed up, filthy inside and out, this truck had chipped paint, a hole where the radio had been cut out and an ignition switch torn from the dashboard—and it now occupied a spot in my upscale neighborhood. But I knew Tasha would grow (oh yes, to a surprising one hundred pounds) and my two-seater sports car wouldn't work much longer for the new us.

Not only did I put this truck on my credit card when I shouldn't have, (What responsible person does that?) but I also started a campaign to "repair" the junk heap.

I used cans of enamel spray paint to color the outside of the truck (tip—that doesn't work). I fixed the heater by inserting screws and splicing wires, guessing which ones should connect. I cut my finger to the bone while trying to jimmy a hydraulic hinge so I could open my door. Into woman-powered restoration, I moved ahead. Why didn't Daddy teach his girl auto mechanics? Tasha was tied a few feet away, interested in the other world she couldn't reach. Meanwhile, I plunged further into fixing up this rubbish.

To my amazement, Tasha reveled in the grungy truck. She'd lie on the seat I had layered with carpets to protect her from the protruding springs. She didn't even try to escape when the door opened; she knew it was *hers*.

My attitude about trucks shifted; I smiled at construction workers, gardeners and those in other trades I now related to; we were living a simple life stripped of stress, just doing what we wished, on our time. Like me, these other truck drivers often also had panting dogs hanging out their car windows.

I now saw Silicon Valley professionals as snobs—people who wasted their lives striving to earn money, obtain status and accumulate possessions that might not matter. They were lifeless blobs. Maybe I was a bit obsessed. I should know—I used to be one of them, but since finding Tasha I was beginning to gain some perspective on what was actually necessary in life.

I took Tasha everywhere, and she patiently waited in *her* truck while I stopped and did my life. It was a real contrast to her feistiness when I worked my long 10 hour days and would return home to her puppy rage. She'd nip at me, chew up tissues and attack anything not tacked down to get her "mamma's" attention. This would go on for three hours before she'd finally exhaust herself and fall asleep on my warm lap.

Looking back, it was worth it to put up with her outbursts. In return, I had a constant supporter for years, this changer of my life course.

In the beginning, she lived through long days at my demanding jobs and the coming and going of boyfriends. She comforted me when each relationship ended. She even survived our numerous camping trips, which she hated perhaps because of the wild animal cries we heard and the subzero temps we endured at night.

She saw the full array of my emotions—tears, laughter,

depression, elation. Ever steady, she held me with her mind and eyes in calm repose. She then put up with the loss of *us* when I would leave many times for lengthy international travels, but Tasha always welcomed me home, forgiving my absence.

When she was a year old, we needed a different environment from our hectic city and moved to a small mountain town in Idaho where she could roam and I could live the simple life.

As Tasha began to age, she started having some health issues. She reached a point where she could barely stand due to her increasing dysplasia. She'd trip on her favorite red ball, fear in her eyes as she'd spread-eagle. I'd rush to her. She'd roll over and over in horror, trying to regain her composure. Then she'd stop, resolved to her fate and waiting for rescue.

I tried to make light of the situation, offering reassurance with my upbeat tone and moving yet one more rug under her body for traction. She seemed to look into my encouraging eyes, at first doubting but then finding hope. I knew I'd have to make a decision soon—not for me but for Tasha. Of course, I wanted to keep her alive as long as possible, but more importantly, I wanted her to die with dignity.

Toward the end, her pain frequently caused her to whimper. Her sad amber eyes seemed to plead with me. She shook. She stopped eating and drinking. Her weight dropped 25 percent.

The three days preceding the veterinary appointment to end her life presented moments of pleasure, a time of giving and receiving. I cried, and she acknowledged the depth of my sorrow by nuzzling me with her now dry nose. To provide a buffer against the winter chill, I lit fires and we sat together in front of the warm glow, enjoying this time of togetherness. I gave her special treats, scraps, when I could coax her into eating a bit. I laid rugs down throughout the house and took her on walks that had once thrilled her, though now she could only stand for a short while. We shared close times of *us*. During these final days, I stayed home to be by her side. I slept next to her on the floor when she couldn't stand; my body wrapped hers in a nest of warmth.

I think she would have agreed with my final decision to give her dignity, to rob her of pain and suffering.

The day I euthanized my pet, the most difficult challenge of my life had arrived. I did not accompanied my previous dog, Sunshine, into the room where they put her down for fear I might cry uncontrollably, embarrass myself or feel too much pain. This time I realized I must go in. Tasha had given me so much; I owed it to her to be brave and comfort her in the last moments of life.

She lay down on a warm fluffy blanket and two office assistants injected her with pentobarbital. We all talked to her in soothing tones and caressed her into oblivion. She calmed down, slipped peacefully away as a woof of air escaped her body, pushing my hands upward. It symbolized her rising. It was an unexpected healing experience.

Two nights later, a feeling of urgency surfaced that I didn't understand. I was in my jammies, but I needed to get out of bed and go outside, into a blizzard. I took a path through the woods that Tasha had once enjoyed. I talked to her one last time, told her I adored her and would now release her to go play up in doggie heaven and chase a fox.

Now it was her time to romp forward to another world. I had guided and enabled her on this journey, but she became *my* guide, helping me become a more courageous person.

"Courage is the act that surpasses the feeling of fear," says *Daegan Smith*.

The next story is about my friend Bob's heartrending journey. Many of us will be affected by Alzheimer's disease during our lives, either directly or indirectly through family or friends. With the right perspective and with the assistance of our angels, a positive experience can emerge.

Why Me? A Family's Struggle with Alzheimer's

Not a fun two days: Bob was suffering, his wife Rita was suffering and as I entered their world—I now suffered.

Fifteen years ago, Bob and Rita had loaded only the possessions that fit in their truck and had ventured to the mountains of Montana to escape their home in smog-laden California. A cowboy retired from city life, Bob reassured his wife, who always followed him. "We are going to a wonderful place to live and emotionally settle; where we belong." It would be their paradise in a pocket of clear skies, a home with good neighbors and room for their horses.

This is Bob's story.

It must have started years before any of us, including Bob, actually thought anything of it. I remember him showing some signs that he was struggling with memory, but we dismissed them for years—maybe five. At first, no one talked about this. Then it became too obvious not to.

Ten years after they arrived at their pristine homestead, *it* struck. That unwelcomed visitor—Alzheimer's disease. It was shocking to see it invade Bob's close-knit blissful family without invitation. At first, the disease was a sudden, partner slipping in discreetly, disguised as peace and calm. Then it became more aggressive, eventually creating havoc.

Who takes responsibility for this invasion and outcome?

At times friendly, at times abhorrent, this disease would not leave. All we could do was watch in disbelief, and if possible, reluctantly accept.

It ravished Bob's brain and the unity of their family. They questioned where they might go for help to rid themselves of this insidious plague.

I visited the homestead to see how Bob and his wife were managing. What I saw was the potent bond that had grown throughout their forty-five year marriage, the crux of this couple.

As I sat in a chair opposite them, I witnessed a unique sharing between the two. She stood behind her seated husband, stroking his sliver-gray hair to calm him or maybe herself. Perhaps she was trying to conjure strength for the both of them. I had never seen her do this before — it appeared adoration flowed from her hands, appreciation for a man who had always been so defiant and in control during their lifetime.

She kissed his head, his cheeks knowing this display of affection would not last forever — a fleeting connection they had finally discovered.

There would never be another caregiver allowed in their lives, she said. This was her place in marriage, her commitment to care for this blessed man, despite how difficult it might prove to be.

Stage two of Alzheimer's disease — that unwelcome host — continued to invade the family space, now more intrusively.

How would Bob, and his loving wife Rita, deal with his medical challenges on this remote acreage? How would they manage the financial cost? In reality, how long could Rita care for her cherished husband before he would have to go to a care center?

He wished to have his spurs, saddle, country vest and silver buckle to rest in his bedroom—and grave. He knew his body was dying.

The disease progressed. He saw men invading his domain, horrible blobs dripping from the ceiling, aggressive ants attacking and scurrying across his wood floor. He'd stomp on their hiding places, holes he imagined in the floor. "Shouldn't I plug these holes?" he asked. He witnessed mice taking control of his living room, venturing to and fro, wherever, whenever they wished. One day he called for us because he said they were moving his ottoman from beneath.

Occasionally, Bob, Rita and I would find pleasure and humor in this difficult progression of his disease, but he was minimally cognizant of his new reality. Occasionally he experienced moments of complete lucidity, infusing false hope—a cruel player in this disease.

Sixteen miles away, a fire began to rage, almost surrounding their homestead. Recent years of low precipitation had left their yellow mark on the property's wheatgrass. But a fire also raged inside him.

Soon it was Rita's birthday. The end of the day often triggered Bob's sundowner symptoms that included the surreal images from another world. He'd become more agitated, more confused. Where was he—what room, what city, what state, what time of existence in his mind? Given Bob's state and the threat of fall fires looming on the periphery of their isolated community, Rita's birthday dinner would probably be popcorn and a stiff gin to cope.

Aware of the fire, Bob wanted us to scout the perimeter of his land and then drive to the main road and see if flames were close. He was agitated, with little ability to distinguish truth from fiction. All occurrences were major events out of his control. Bob was progressing down a path of no options.

His days and nights were no longer distinguishable—a mishmash of the unbelievable. Now there were men outside his, yes *his* home, in hunting jackets—scurrying surreptitiously on the property.

He was the man, the defender, the man who fixed whatever needed fixing. "Where are the guns—even one of the many I own?" Bob wanted to protect himself and his wife. If he could just find one, that would scare them, stop them from the invasion his imagination acknowledged.

When we were going to inspect his property, he remembered where he had hid one of his thirty guns. His family had tried to secretly remove some of the guns, but he still managed to get hold of one that he'd tucked away. About to survey the fires, he showed me what he had found—a weapon to defend.

With courage, I challenged the gun, trying to prevent an accident. "No one gets in my car with a gun," I asserted.

Perhaps recalling my fervent distain for guns, he looked me in the eyes as he raised his eyebrows. He studied my face one last time before dropping the pewter barrel loaded with two bullets on the speckled granite kitchen counter.

The next day, Bob wanted his wife to stop working so hard, for a moment, just a moment, to reunite in the sun.

She relinquished her challenging schedule and sat with her husband in their weathered chairs; the afternoon sun illuminated their faces as they looked out on the serene prairie. A decision she will never regret.

Devastation struck later in the week. Rita worked in their shop; Bob left the house by himself. A perfect day for a stroll, he must have thought (in his state, a shuffle down the dirt path).

Something interfered with his plans and his body fell to the scorched earth. He lay in the sun for more than two hours, unaware of the threat. He foamed at the mouth, cradled by the ground he loved.

His wife opened the door to their cozy home at day's end. She searched for the man who always sat in his chair. Frantically she rushed through their house, then outside, where she came upon his body. She called an ambulance and watched them load her man inside the sterile bowels of the rescue vehicle.

The piercing sun had penetrated his essence and caused a seizure, which accelerated his hallucinations. In the hospital, they learned that Bob had Lewy body dementia, not Alzheimer's exclusively. Symptoms of this disease include seeing family members as imposters and suffering horrific delusions, now a reality in his hellish ethereal world.

What an existence I would not wish on anyone, as snakes invaded his world while his wife and I sipped coffee. I felt this was a torturous conundrum without a way to head off possible disaster given the hidden guns still on the premises.

His delusions, the men, and now one woman, propagated on his ranch all the time. He saw their shapes, one with each leg the size of his now slight frame, as they took over his home, sitting in his favorite chair. He moved to another chair, not daring to disrespect them. The territory became theirs. He was now *their* guest for as long as his illusions allowed him to stay in his home that they occupied.

I saw and felt the horror of his experiences, the inability of his wife to reassure him that what he saw wasn't real; her existence seemed cursed, too. No person should die like this.

I grieved so deeply for this couple that at times it was difficult for me to function. Exhausted after endless worries, sleepless nights and listless days, I did not want to engage in my normal activities. I even withdrew from friendships. I felt imprisoned behind barbed wire in a concentration camp of my mind, stripped bare of my essence. My moroseness grew. I felt numb and guilty for my life of gratitude.

I was terrified and helpless—terrified because of those guns and helpless because it was not my battle to fight. I struggled during the dark hours; nightmares wouldn't let go. I cried. I tried to find comfort in any way I could—eating and drinking—but nothing helped. I realized the depth of my feelings, that I could not control this situation. A positive outcome remained elusive as I wrestled with my own emotions about the situation.

In my desperation to help Bob as his disease progressed, I found a way to help. I promised him my angels would come to protect him and ease his agony. I worked with my spirits daily, focusing their voyage to his home and clarifying their mission. He called a couple days later, desperate they had still not arrived to assist him in his battles.

I scolded them, explaining the difficulty of the assignment and how they needed to try harder. I sent pictures of these stunning angels to his wife who placed them in their home where he could be reminded of their presence. I hoped the pictures would help him visualize them.

It took a while for any results to manifest, but on numerous calls he thanked me and spoke of their protection and help.

Although my angels assisted Bob, his disease was too immersed in his mind to avoid the next disaster. What a hurricane, well, maybe a tornado. Bob and Rita went to stay with their daughters' families two states away. No one slept as Bob acted out. They were worn to their limit. It escalated; Bob reacted negatively to his son-in-law, not recognizing him. The ghouls had overtaken his mind and possibly his wife's body, he thought. A knight, he would defend against the ones that wanted her.

Sally's angel

He was a man with one mission—to protect, though he had no real weapons. Soon he crossed over even family boundaries by attacking his son-in-law during the perfectly planned birthday celebration for Bob's eighty good years of adventures. Too much stimulation and noise had created a storm that set him off.

With unexpected strength, he picked up a chair and threw it at his son-in-law. Plates and glass shattered. Then he pulled off the linens and attacked his other devoted son-in-law.

The party had gone terribly wrong as Bob tried to protect his family. Someone called 911, and when the paramedics arrived, they wrestled Bob onto a stretcher as he shouted to his wife, "Leave me, save yourself."

Rita stared at this man, the pinnacle of her and their children's world, the one she turned to for every decision in their lives. "Bob, please tell me what to do!" But he did not answer. She was on her own.

Rita relayed to me what happened at the celebration, and I realized he was not far from death. During meditation, I saw this man on a horse, his stature erect as he rode up to those I love in their wonderful paradise. The heavenly environment I created in my mind had emerald-green trees filtering sunlight, blue-green water rushing. Appearing through the trees, Bob rode up to the scene, feeling blissful during his daily visit to the river's edge. All was in full color as I viewed the others who have passed.

An angel said to me, "He is not with us yet in heaven. This is wrong," and suddenly his image warped to a transparent gray. *Do they get the play wrong in heaven?* During each subsequent morning meditation and blessing, he now appeared gray. It was not his time yet, but maybe the universe was preparing him to cross over to this more permanent ecstasy.

When Bob arrived at the hospital after the party incident, Rita explained to me that the doctors who treated him did not understand his Lewy body dementia and injected him with medication for schizophrenia. He had an adverse reaction to it; his violence and agitation increased. The hospital wanted him gone but a long-term care center, his last hope, said they would try to accommodate him *if* he was calm.

Bob raged during the three-hour transport. When he arrived, the door opened and Bob saw new faces, maybe kinder than those from the hospital and the images imprinted in his memory from his long battle.

He immediately relaxed, walked for the first time in days and entered the soothing, dimly lit lobby with a welcoming fireplace at its center. Positive, calm vibes emanated from the building and slowly, one by one, residents' doors opened. A woman whispered to the others about the new person who would be staying with them. They seemed to delight in a stranger's entrance into their world.

You could hear Bob screaming, "Rita, Rita, Rita," as they tried to get him settled. He was told she was going away for awhile. (The facility had instructed Rita not to visit for a few days so he could get used to his new environment.) He appeared confused. "But, she always comes!" And she had for all of their marriage. Life would change for both of them as they learned to separate and start new paths.

At the long-term care center, Bob's hallucinations increased to the point where he violently threw furniture. After each rage subsided, he apologized to the nurses, explaining that he didn't want to act this way. He pleaded with them, expressing his wish to die *now*.

When Rita returned for a visit, she entered the room before other family members. Both she and Bob cried tears of joy and contentment; he finally recognized her.

One by one his daughters arrived, and he greeted each one with the same joyful recognition. For forty-five minutes, he was able to stay in the now, in the real world with his family. How blessed they were with this exchange, until the light left. Eventually, his eyes glossed over, and Bob once again departed to the "other world," the house of horrors.

This exchange was a gift to each of them, providing an unexpected opportunity to reconnect with the father and husband they loved. It is strange how recognition from someone precious in your life affects you. It's not something you think about it until it's no longer possible. These moments acknowledge who you are, where and how you belong in the other's life; it's extremely fulfilling.

While Bob and his family received this gift of a meaningful exchange, I stopped at a comfortable coffeehouse after dropping my daughter and grandchildren at the airport. They had visited from another state to care for and cheer me up after extensive facial surgery. After they left, I was hesitant to look in the mirror at my newly arranged face. The third day, alone, I changed the dressings, time to address what I would see in the mirror. It was hideous. There were three long vertical slashes that stretched under my lip and one long horizontal cut above my chin. My lip was now drawn upward on the right at a strange angle, with erratic cuts running where you'd never expect them.

Always looking for the positive, I smiled inside (not supposed to use facial gesture for some time); my face resembled a tic-tac-toe board. The surgeon had meticulously worked on the suturing for forty-five minutes so I knew it wouldn't be pretty.

What I saw could possibly, eventually, be acceptable — the new me. I'd need to concoct an astounding story of a life adventure to explain this unusual sight. A bear had gotten me in a tent, had swung its long claws and ripped flesh from my face. Or on one of my trips to Turkey, I had been captured and tortured; my face cut. Or I had been paddling down the Amazon, fishing for piranha when the dugout tipped and I fell into the water where a frenzy of orange man (in this case woman) eaters swiftly attacked my face.

The trips were real—not these mishaps and not how this face got rearranged.

So here I was in the café, sitting on a cushy velvet sofa, surrounded by vibrant art as I sipped my favorite coffee through a straw for the first time in a week. I barely could move my lips because of the stitches but was still enjoying that familiar taste of my beverage and the calm of my surroundings when my cell phone rang, jarring my tranquility.

It was Rita. She explained that Bob had just entered

the hospice program. He might die within a few days or linger two weeks, but surely the end was imminent. He was no longer eating or drinking. She said he was a skeleton with little water reserve to sustain him. She felt this was voluntary on his part.

My stomach tightened. I went numb.

Two weeks prior to Rita's phone call, Bob told Rita that he—who did not appear to be a religious man—had seen Jesus. "Oh," Rita asked, "how was he dressed?"

"He was in one piece of cloth and explained he would assist me." (Get to heaven?) Bob could only mumble now, but he attempted to whisper the carefully formed words to get his point understood.

Eighteen months from when we acknowledged Bob's Alzheimer's symptoms, he and his family's torture was over. Rita and one of their daughters spent the day with him. In the afternoon, his other daughter arrived and called her siblings who lived out of state to let them know the end was imminent. On the phone, one of his daughters sang the song she had held in her heart her whole life. Another daughter told Bob she was releasing him; he could go to heaven when he was ready.

This particular phase took all of their courage. Rita sang Bob his last song, spoke of her feelings for him and gave him permission to leave.

Five minutes into the families' drive home, the phone rang. Bob had died. He was released from his torture on earth and now would ascend.

But not yet.

One daughter screamed, "Let me out of the car. He is here right now." When the car stopped, she ran into her home, grabbed her kids, and went back outside. They looked up at the stars, raised their hands to feel his presence.

He probably hung around for a bit, as my Michael did with me, then went on to paradise. Relationships never end. When that person you adore is no longer on earth, you must be sure not to abuse the connection and request they stay too long or come too often as they return briefly to support you. With gratitude, you celebrate your time with this person while on earth and beyond.

Rita sent me this message a month later:

When Bob passed, he left us with his energy to move forward in life; new beginnings to get us through life and I am absolutely positive he ascended to sit with God and meet Jesus. Through Bob's earlier religious practices and his continued, but previously silent belief in God, he is now by his side.

One daughter took her mom to the nursery to buy a dogwood tree. Rita craves color, something ready to bloom as spring approaches. She wished to nourish life, plant beauty in her world, so long absent.

This is a painful story for me to recount because I cared so deeply for this couple and have been angry something so devastating separated their love. But, after coming to accept Bob's death, I can see some glimpses of beauty, laughter we three allowed ourselves to share at times and the possibility that angels did intervene to soften the difficulty of his journey. We never know what is real when we can't see an earthly image, but maybe the angels were with Bob to the end and guided him to his next home in heaven, along with Jesus.

Chapter 5
Vision Quest

*"In silence you hear who you are becoming.
You create yourself."*

Jewel

A VISION QUEST MARKS A SIGNIFICANT TRANSITION IN LIFE. Vision quests are a rite of passage that many native cultures practice throughout the world. These sacred events can touch a spark of light within, separating us from the ordinary world. They can create a special place we return to for sustenance and centering.

The delicate spring blooms were moving in unison, pushed by a crisp, fresh breeze. A few patches of earth and green were surfacing through the snowmelt. Billows of white puffs slowly drifted through the heavens. I saw shapes—angels, animals and people in the sky. Near me, a white-tailed deer family was running through the remaining snow. They were full of life, frolicking as one; they did not even notice my presence.

On this day, I took a leap into the unknown.

People have searched for direction, for purpose, and to unite with God and Spirit for ages. In 500 BCE, Buddha went into the forest and fasted under the Bodhi Tree. Christ fasted in the desert, Moses climbed Mount Sinai and Mohammed went into a cave.

American Indians frequently participate in a four-day ceremony that starts in a sweat lodge. Then they move into the woods or embark on a voyage for several days to find enlightenment. There is no eating or sleeping during this time. Prayers, meditation and cries to their sacred source prepare people for a vision. Those who participate in this quest feel protected by their spirit animal or nature as a revelation, or dream, reveals their purpose in life and how they can perform community service to assist others.

An American Indian Ogala holy man, Black Elk, described such a quest. Black Elk climbed the sacred mountain and once he was there, he saw a thread of smoke — it was the cord that connects us to the creator and from which all is created. He saw all the threads emanating outward, and he knew it was the center of the universe.

He then prayed to the four directions: West for rest and reflection, North for patience and purity, East for energy and emotions and South for discipline and direction. He gave thanks, for without these elements we could not live, and then thanked the creator for his knowledge and gifts.

I had always questioned what a journey into the mind would involve, and now motivated by writing this book, I realized it could give me insight I could relay to others and possibly provide an expanded glimpse into my life's purpose and direction. I would conduct my own abbreviated quest, a day at home. (I didn't have the time to take a long journey or a way to venture into some snow-covered remote area.)

This quest appealed to me because I felt an intense connection with native folklore. I thought the experience would be a benign challenge in my world. I knew little about the process so I made up my own rules; it's not the first time in life that I have done that.

I felt surprisingly uneasy about this simple adventure into . . . what or where? I did not know. The day before my quest, I asked myself, *How should I do this thing*? I've never heard of anyone embarking on a citified, short excursion into their soul.

I would not consume food for forty hours, only nonalcoholic liquids. (I did allow myself an eight-ounce health smoothie that helped with hunger, energy and hydration.) I would not bring a clock or watch with me, judging time only by the angle of the sun or by noting light or darkness. This was particularly difficult. I desire to see the time displayed and feel slightly off balance when it is not available. I would only use my plastic-enclosed patio without heat, or I would roam outdoors. I would allow myself quick potty breaks inside the house. There would be no communication devices or conversations with people. No more music. No television. *No Computer!*

I sent a message to family members explaining my short, safe vision quest and asked they not contact me during this time. My mother commented, "Oh Sally, you are getting so weird." I guess that is one way to describe my searches and curiosities in life. I never heard back from the others I communicated with almost daily. I speculated they were on vacation, involved in a life crisis, didn't care or also thought my "weirdness" had surfaced again and didn't want to talk to me at this moment. Focused, I shifted to my quest: I would meditate, play some aboriginal musical instruments and try to stay awake, if possible.

I ceased eating April 2 at 5:00 pm and then April 3 at 9:00 am I began preparing for my quest by taking a steamy shower to signify sitting in a sweat lodge. I put on a wonderful CD by Brooke Medicine Eagle called *Gathering: The Sacred Breath*. Intuitively, my daughter had given me this CD of American Indian music last year. My thoughts were full of gratitude as I did my yoga and then assumed a meditative position on my porch with only the bare essentials.

My stomach growled, but I refused to acknowledge it wanted food. Now in my primeval state, I attempted to impose the rules of my vision quest. I read the temperature gage on the wall of this enclosure: forty degrees. Ted, a friend of mine, had built this room as a surprise for me while I was away on a camping trip. Home a bit earlier than he expected, I found him hammering and nail gunning, attempting to finish before my return. It was his gesture of appreciation and caring.

On the Persian carpet I loved, patterned in warm burnt orange and black, rested a timeworn rocker barely held together with glue. Lining one wall in this room were stacks of wood to burn in my house, a buffer against the chilling winter temps. As I decorated and used this room, it became me, and I gave thanks to that man who gifted it.

I had also planted many seedlings in my view, to improve and softened the monochrome palette of vegetation and flatness. I had longed to enhance the vista when purchasing my home. The real estate agent had said, "Oh, don't worry about the sparseness—you plant trees." With the strong hands of friends, I had accomplished this over the years, creating a special place where I watched the beauty of sunrises and sunsets. The day filtered warmth into the room that created surprising high temperatures. Nights were chilly, matching the outdoors—cycles of contrast. So now I had achieved a comfortable and satisfying view from the bareness of the original patio.

I inflated my quarter-inch, twenty-five year-old sleeping pad and vowed to replace it this year; it barely lifted my body off the ground. Feeling the moisture of condensation on the patio carpet, I stopped meditating to find my moisture barrier, a blanket I use when camping. Unfortunately, it was buried in a hard to reach spot behind my garaged car. I squeezed by it, found a bit of comfort I'd enjoy with this rubber-lined blanket and slowly moved back into meditation after arranging my sleeping bag.

I spotted a plant in the corner of the room that I had recently watered in the hopes that hydration would start to send green spring growth above the brown soil. It could be in my way, so I got up and moved the plant to an unoccupied corner. But when I looked down, I saw brown water dripping from the planter, saturating my rug and sleeping bag. Oh dear, it could be a very uncomfortable night.

I set out my flashlight, made a thermos of ice water, brought tissues, grabbed a change of clothes—I had no idea what for—and arranged my musical instruments, rocks and feathers—my passions—on the floor, along with a diary. Wow, what a lot of work to meditate, or something like that, for this day.

What time was it? How much longer would I have to wait for darkness? How could I even tell? Then I rationalized that my body would convey that information to me. Besides, did it matter? This was *my* quest, until the sun rose tomorrow and slightly warmed my porch.

My stomach wouldn't stop growling—it was not used to missing breakfast or any meal. For a fleeting second, I considered how much I adored food. Then I censored that thought, worried I would start contemplating what evening cocktail or wine I'd choose to accompany what I'd eat.

Not getting into the reflective thing, I went for a slow, long, meaningful walk toward the woods at the end of my street. As I planted each boot in the snow, I realized there were spring scents I had never noticed before—a mixture of melting snow and moist ground preparing to release its abundance. I heard returning birds singing joyful songs, trying to identify and attract a mate. I heard woodpeckers' drum roll as they foraged for delicious insect morsels in wood and squirrels screeching for no apparent reason as they moved to the new rhythm of spring. Finally, I stopped thinking about the preparations for my quest and begin to immerse myself in it.

At the trail end, I found an abandoned house. I brushed sand and stones off an adjacent ledge and sat there for an hour looking at the trees, letting my mind spin in disorganized relaxation. I stared at the snowmelt. I don't think I had ever done that before, watch snow melt; it was very hypnotic. The droplets released from glittering crystals changed property, drenching the partially exposed dirt and merging into puddles. First, bulky rocks launched down the hill randomly. Gravel soon followed as earth awakened and began its transformation.

The sun softly kissed my face and a breeze, ever so slight, tickled me in my relaxed state. I wished to be naked, enjoying these senses with all of my body, even in the snow.

Nature, the element that connects my life, offered me repose and I accepted it with thankfulness.

Reluctant to leave the gifts of Mother Nature, I carried some of them home to my patio: a smooth white rock, a perfect, tightly closed oblong pinecone and a fallen spruce branch resembling a delicate broom.

Drawn to remain outside in the sun's warmth, I found a green spot between some trees where the snow had melted in my yard. I brought an orange-and-yellow, nylon-striped beach chair and footstool outside, positioned them close to the pine trees for a cozy shelter and maneuvered so I could view my snowcapped mountain, rimmed by deep blue sky. Wisps of clouds started to form in preparation for the imminent storm that would lower the temperature to the twenties and probably bring a dusting of snow for the night.

Two robins landed next to me in a tree where they enjoyed the end to winter's harshness. They didn't expect a human to be in their playground. Before they flew away, I delighted in their essence, the vibrant breast of the male and the muted brown of the female. Never had I been this close to robins before. Less than two feet away, I was mesmerized by their beauty, usually viewed from within my house.

Blessed to live in a sparsely settled area with few homes, people and cars and little noise, I pretended to be in my splendid forests that I journey to by car or hike to as often as possible.

More clouds accumulated; in wonder, I watched their slow formation. The snow sparkled and continued to release its moisture to nourish new sprouts. The evergreens sent up new shoots of brilliant green, as if to say, "Look at me! How I perform to beautify the world." Pinecones were developing at each branch tip, adding to the sense of renewal. Buds of adjacent trees swelled, soon to burst with greens to dress naked branches.

Suddenly, my attention was redirected toward an animal with rust-colored fur scampering past me. This winter fox was on a mission. Fully dressed in a winter coat, the fox was soon to be looking scrawny in summer's heat. His golden colors contrasted with the ice-white snow as he scurried in search of food, a mate, joy. Who knew?

I thought about how the foxes had diminished in the sixteen years I had occupied my property. When I first moved here, I enjoyed an abundance of elk, deer and even lynx. But the number of houses multiplied, to my chagrin; I only paid for my patch of earth so I was not able to control my surroundings. It filled me with sorrow to see the animals disappear. Where did they go? Did hunters, with their constant fall target practice, destroy them or were the animals smart enough to stay away when they heard and smelled the bullets? Our natural environment is a rhythm we should always celebrate and protect.

A transplant from the cement sidewalks and crime-laden high-rises of Silicon Valley, I remembered my first winter here in this remote gem of a town. The previous owner of my mountain home had fed an egg to a fox each day and instructed me, if I wished, to continue. I did not. In my mind, you never feed wildlife; otherwise you upset the natural balance of their ecosystem.

When I moved in, the momma fox came for several days and sat outside my French doors creating a ruckus—my dog, inside, smelled a wild animal she could not catch. No egg for this begging mom. Then she got smart. One day, she led her baby kit right up to the door, somehow instructing it to stay as she sauntered off. Now, confronted by one very cute baby fox looking up at me, what could I do? Soon I opened the door, offering an egg. This experience was never repeated, because I felt it should not be, but, oh, how I laughed at the cunning mom.

I still enjoyed being among wildlife, but instead of seeing animals like that momma fox in the light of day, which saddened me, I saw the evidence—their footprints and droppings—that they had visited during the night.

I checked the angle of the sun; it must be noon so time to treat myself to a sip of my smoothie—banana, grape and a hint of chocolate. I noted the amazing taste, the slight texture to the liquid and the zing of caffeine ebbing through my veins with delight, such a simple pleasure made special by the absence of food.

This sacred place under the trees of my yard, as I now refer to it, is protected, secluded from neighbors and the wind. I had never considered sitting here before. I slowed down and finally connected to everything around me. Moving to this mountain had taught me how to live a more relaxed life and how to eliminate possessions and desire; however, I still strived each day for goals. I realized that most of that striving might not be necessary for happiness. I seldom allowed myself to sit in stillness and surrender. This day, I gave myself that gift. *This day, April 3, 2016, I give myself permission to just be.*

Alerted to a sound I didn't want to hear, I saw a woodpecker perched high on my house having a wonderful time disassembling the wood on my chase above my very steep, twelve-pitch metal roof. Who would fix that demolition? I had never heard a woodpecker on my property, but usually I lived indoors where there is little sound. I scolded him as he flew away to an adjacent tree, alerting his mate. Peeking around pine needles, he is dressed with a red hat and has a striking black and white torso. He squawked at me in defiance as the couple flew off toward my mountain. *May they find other wood to destroy.*

I stopped fuming and enjoyed their beauty. I chose forgiveness over being upset, with acceptance.

Clouds moved quicker now, forming feathery stripes, then puffs. I heard a waterfall of melting snow under my patio. Fearful, I wondered where the water would settle—below my house where it had flooded years ago? Oh well. It sounded like a waterfall if you put your mind in the right place so I considered that. An occasional doggie barked to let me know I remained in civilization.

I realized what this tranquility reminded me of. It was similar to when you are sick. You lie on your favorite comfy couch covered with a soft blanket. If you are lucky enough to have a loving person nursing you back to health, they might bring you warm chicken soup. That was what I was experiencing, but nature was doing the nurturing, bringing me comfort.

I became gratitude, with all my being.

If I did this quest for three or four days instead of one, might it result in expanding appreciation?

My world was now this tree cluster. Many different birds dropped by, taking a look at the odd woman with a baseball cap and cowboy boots lounging on a chair.

I saw images in the cloud formations again, a pleasure I had experienced when I was nine. My sister, brother and I would lie on our backs nestled in sweet-smelling clover, just being kids. On this day, I still saw images in those clouds—a cute, pudgy teddy bear reclining on its back, paws nestling his face, his mamma racing to him.

My attention centered on the hand-pressed paper I was writing on, noticing for the first time all the colors and texture on the pages in this book I've written in through the years. Monsieur red-headed woodpecker found his way back. Perched in the tree next to me, he again peeked around a branch. He is stunning; maybe it is all right he stays.

A steak, and, yes, a loaded baked potato with a superb cabernet sauvignon—possibly a 1991—would be perfect, I mused. But I wouldn't trade my current bliss for that, absolutely not. I was exactly where I should be at this moment.

The noise of a plane intruded upon my repose. It should not have been in my paradise. But I accepted it, just as it disappeared to places where others wouldn't notice the noise or care if they did.

I glanced at the ground peppered with holes from the voles, mice and snakes living beneath my feet. How would it be to live in their dark cities, only surfacing at times to see the surrounding light of greenery and white-blue skies?

Reading some of my earlier journal entries about my arrival and struggles in McCall, I realized how lonesome I felt after leaving my friends and not knowing anyone here. I had long gotten over that. I reflected on those changes where I found my being—my environment, my people here in this small town. I was where I should be at this moment in time. It was so perfect and I wondered how that happens in life. Maybe through searching, you accept what is offered at that moment. To stop, feel and love.

A sandhill crane flew overhead with his mate for life. These big, awkward-looking birds become graceful in flight, the same ones returning to their nest across the street by the lake each year.

I took a long walk around my subdivision, up and down hills, through trees and neighborhoods. I met a couple down the street setting up their Chalet RV, and they offered to show me how it worked. They counseled me on options for my future trips, suggesting I look into a class B vehicle where I could sleep, not their Chalet, that would require towing. Did they suspect my driving skills challenges? I hesitated to talk with them, but, after all, when an opportunity to learn knocked on this rural city vision quest, I decided to answer—so we talked a short time, then I left them, wondering why I had rushed off.

I walked toward the river, but when seeing a woman and her dog, I changed directions to avoid another conversation. Earlier, I had been unable to avoid a discussion with my next-door neighbor. When I sat outside, he came over to talk. It wasn't so easy to have this solitary quest in my home environment—that's why people went elsewhere I suspected.

Once home, away from all those social interactions I was attempting to avoid, I tried to meditate on my now warm patio with sun streaming in. According to the gauge, the temperature had risen to 110 degrees. I was dripping with sweat. I did my best to concentrate. It didn't work. Bored, I entered my house and did a labyrinth walk while reciting affirmations to myself.

After my quest, I did some research about the labyrinth, a circular, single spiral that leads you in and out a particular path. It is a symbol of wholeness and a metaphor for a journey to the center of your deepest self as you move out into the world with a broader understanding of who you are.

Not sure what to do as I embarked on my spiral walk, I began chanting and shaking my Peruvian gourd. Being active was a better state for me when I found it difficult to sit still, but the quest was stillness, an adventure into your deeper self, and solace I believe.

I then read more of my diary. Forgotten events resurfaced and generated new meaning. I read about conflicts from the past and realized how much progress I had made over the past sixteen years, a period of time when I was floundering to identify my life's purpose and deal with the accumulated guilt I felt.

Every time I left my daughter's home, guilt surfaced. I would not be near to support her or greet my grandchildren when they returned home from school. I would not be able to guide them through their difficulties. But I needed my mountain environment. I couldn't stay for long periods, but feeling a desire to be with my family, I became a gypsy, traveling south frequently throughout each year.

The sun would set in a couple hours; the porch would

cool and I would get into my sleeping bag for what I imagined would be a long, chilly night.

Maybe I had gotten this vision quest out of my system; possibly I should be alone in the woods or on a walking quest. I committed to continuing until morning, but I'd be elated when the sun rose and I was done with this.

Darkness approached and the temperature dropped dramatically. I finished reading my diary filled with sad memories. In 2006, I had written about an upsetting, actually frightening, reoccurring dream. Clutching an ax covered with blood, my ex-husband pursued me with the intention to kill. I ran to save myself; this fear consumed me. In the dream I was filled with anxiety, wondering how I might warn our daughter so she could save herself.

I experienced a similar real life fear during her childhood, when I left her at home with him. I feared he might hurt her but rationalized he wouldn't. Wasn't he her father? How could he? However, there were frequent red handprints on her butt when I returned.

The answer was immediately apparent when I read this diary entry about my terrifying dream. It was quite simple. A mother saves her child before herself, a discovery I'd made too late. I lived with this fear of my ex hurting me and our daughter ever since she'd been born, but I was very lucky that my daughter's benevolence allowed me to make reparation in many ways. I didn't know if she had forgiven me at this juncture, but she certainly made me feel honored to be her mother. The most difficult part was forgiving myself.

With our imperfections, we are human; the most important thing we can do is learn from our mistakes and in the future make better, more loving decisions.

Other entries in my diary were about my attempt to

rescue a friend from his self-destructive behavior—an interesting read on how not to live your life (mine). But I had learned from those years, frustrated with my inability to fulfill my goal of saving this man. I now understood when to help and when to withdraw. I learned to set my boundaries.

I could barely see outside, but I was able to distinguish a brown spec dashing erratically in front of my porch and entering its home below the patio where I lay. Now, that gave my night a completely different perspective.

I plugged in the miniature white Christmas lights that emit a soft glow. I covered up with an electric blanket, justifying this extravagance because I couldn't possibly build a fire to enjoy the flickers and warmth unless in the woods. Was I cheating?

The cranes flew overhead, returning to their nest as night closed in. Peace, serenity and a twinge of hunger filled my stomach.

Tomorrow: *Food!*

I spied a vole—wilderness Sal knew it was not a mouse because it lacked a tail. He emerged from his night's lodging to get a better look at me; this lady under a red blanket was a strange occurrence. Then again, maybe he was seeking warmth under my soft covers. I tapped on the plastic window hoping to frighten him away. He just stared at me.

Suddenly, I saw what could be more nocturnal rodents. Could they squeeze through the one-quarter-inch slats of the floor? Oh goodness. It might be better to experience this in complete darkness so I could not see their movements, only hear them. Flashlight in hand, I'd illuminate the creatures when I heard them. My past boredom had transformed into curiosity.

I did fall asleep late into the night, despite attempting

to stay awake. When drowsing off, I glanced at the star-studded inky sky. Through the plastic enclosing the porch, I saw an arc of stars making a smooth half circle. Was this the arc my editor constantly referred to while I was writing my last book? The glue that would unite all my stories into one cohesive work? Immediately, I saw the word *love* around the stars. Was it a sign to weave the chapters in this book together into a perfectly stitched quilt that would inspire my future readers, guide them to find their highest self?

In the morning, I woke with a smile on my face and in my heart. As I lay in my warm cocoon, the crisp chill surrounding my exposed face, I delighted in listening to the morning bird songs welcome another day. The storm clouds would move in later, but at that moment, the skies were a mixture of eggshell blue and soft pink—a cream with marshmallow clouds.

I would not trade my last day and evening of serenity for anything. I only longed for a bold cup of coffee, no food.

Sadly, I realized I would never see the sunset or sunrise the same, why? I understood I was honoring my first time of *actually* seeing a sunrise, a sunset.

That evening while I sat on my magic patio at sunset, a vole scurried by. It was still light enough to see; I noted his delicate features that no longer threatened. His mate, not ready for their seclusion in the dark, scurried by, picking up leaves, perhaps for their dinner or bed, and then disappeared under my outside patio tarp, the other vole following. Maybe it was a game they played. I saw a wave moving under a canvas until they emerged, jumping on top, claiming their superiority, their right to exist. Then they scampered into their nightspot under my patio.

This journey was not what I had expected—it was so much more. It became my quest into nature where I found the true meaning of my spiritual connection. A connection that resides deep within, a place I can always find solace.*

---

* One option for learning more about vision quests is to visit the School of Lost Borders (www.schooloflostborders.org), which educates and prepares participants who want a modern day vision quest experience in a safe environment.

Chapter 6
Forgiveness

Forgiveness is unlocking the door to set someone free and realizing you were the prisoner!

Max Lucado

FORGIVENESS. THROUGH THE YEARS THE DESIRE TO FORGIVE surfaced, a stab in my heart, but disappeared again just as quickly when I did not act on it. It would have been the positive thing to do, but how to forgive people who have caused damage and been unjust? I knew I should, but I couldn't find a way.

One day, my daughter, Nicole, came to visit me and arrived with something special. As she pulled the book out of her plastic pink suitcase, she casually let it slip from her hand to mine and declared it a present.

I reflected on her recent Christian conversion. She'd had a pool baptism surrounded by friends who'd guided her recent midlife transition. She found a way to release painful memories, surround herself with love and let go of fear. Ever since Nicole accepted God, she was remarkably relaxed and lived in pure joy the majority of the time. She suggested I learn to live in the moment. We aspire to do that, but often we have minefields that are triggered, sabotaging our efforts.

In order to forgive, I learned you must first do the hard work.

I glanced at the book Nicole had given me: *Hand in Hand with God: Finding Your Path to Forgiveness* by Linda Brumley. I hesitated when I read the word *God* and said, "Oh, I will read this when I have time"—I stumbled over my words—"which could be soon after the holiday . . . when I have a moment." She smiled, and I knew she was on a mission.

Organized religion was from my past, no longer anything I related to, and God was not part of my vocabulary.

Sitting in my comfortable cabin environment, I now possibly had the time to tackle this forgiveness thing. But did I have the courage to overcome the barrier I had constructed around my heart, my soul?

Busy with my art and writing, I stalled, rationalizing that I'd put my daughter's book down and tackle it later, someday, when I finished my current projects. In actuality, all these projects would never be done; I constantly embark upon more creative endeavors after each is complete, or before. Did I have the time, or more accurately, did I have the guts to reveal my innermost fears and the energy to move forward and release them?

Thinking about this with a cup of coffee in hand, sitting on my warm porch with the sun streaming in, I realized it would be an act of bravery to move forward. I had learned to navigate trips to far-flung parts of the world, to develop my photography business, my blogs, my writing, but was I ready for a one-on-one confrontation with myself? Why should I do it? What difference would it make in my daily life?

That word *courage* kept surfacing. I suspected my loving daughter purposely gifted this book to me, so after opening the cover, I delved into soft cream-colored pages and started the challenging work to find a way to release past hurts, to forgive.

Here's what I learned initially:

- Small acts of kindness and forgiveness compound daily—pray for blessings for the person you wish to forgive.
- It's useful to wish daily for the perpetrator to have

positive experiences. You might say, "I wish they enjoy blue skies, catch a fish." These affirmations help you develop compassion and positive feelings for the transgressor.
- Compassion turns fear, anger and revenge into forgiveness.
- Buried pain finds no release unless you forgive.
- At first, forgiveness is like going against gravity.

My pain came from many sources: a difficult marriage and subsequent divorce with my ex-husband, two break-ups with ex-boyfriends I didn't initiate or desire and a relative I needed to forgive to dissipate my daily sadness and anger. Forgiveness surfaced with an unquenchable desire to stop reliving occurrences from these relationships that made me feel like a victim.

I acknowledged this fact and began with the goal to redirect my anger and disappointment, offering acceptance and forgiveness to those who had been hurtful. It was not an easy thing to do.

Two of the people I needed to forgive, 1 adored— were dead. What was I supposed to do about that? Dead means dead—gone, no longer there to interact with.

Even before my daughter gave me this book, I had begun the process of forgiveness in my own ineffectual way. But I had been unsuccessful; I still needed to tackle forgiveness so I could move ahead, release and not bury my feelings any longer. After all, I saw those who'd died that I still needed to forgive looking down on me daily as I acknowledged their presence.

One of those people was my ex-boyfriend who'd died unexpectedly several years ago, not unexpectedly for me. When I first met him, he put that stake in the ground and told me when his death would occur—at fifty-five years of age. How could he know precisely when he would die? He did.

The man was my best friend, my soul mate. The relationship was enmeshed with both positive and negative experiences, like most, but ours vacillated between extreme highs and lows. He was an emotionally wounded person who I desperately attempted to influence and change during our eight years together. I tried, I tried and I tried to rescue him, but I never succeeded.

I felt guilty because I could not find the key to unlock a solution. Pain erupted over time. Eventually, I had no positive feelings left to interact with him in a beneficial way. Exhausted, I had run out of my limited vocabulary of assistance. I could not effect a change *in him*. He rejected all I offered; he wanted to live life on his terms.

Near the end of our relationship, there was an incident of betrayal that threatened my survival; I gave up on us. He rebelled. Desperate for my forgiveness, he sought therapy, something he'd always abhorred. One day he brought me a document. It appeared to be four pages of clinical resources and suggestions on how to forgive that he'd received during therapy.

He stated the document's purpose: "I want you to find it in your heart to forgive this major transgression that ended our emotional attachment." I glanced at the pages, those senseless words with no significance for me at the moment. I could not link them to meaningful sentences. They were sterile words on paper. They did not equate with the pain he had caused me, what he had done to me.

"Please, try," he pleaded.

Months later, he confronted me, asked for a hug.

"No," I said. I couldn't, so he raised my arms and held them around his shoulders. It was the best I could do.

At the time, I did not have the tools to forgive him—the pain was too big, too encompassing and too sad for me to face. I was mad. Didn't he understand my pain, what I had gone through for eight years? I was not able to offer the compassion and forgiveness he searched for; we stopped seeing each other romantically, but there was no closure to our relationship. We were in limbo.

Unfortunately, with time, I learned too late how to forgive. Compassion needs to be expansive to reach forgiveness. Why had I lacked this at the time of his need? Why couldn't I have figured this out before he died? Upon learning about his death, I started my in-depth search for celestial learning and connection.

He is in my life daily now and I communicate briefly with him during my morning practice. I send him wishes for glory in paradise and let him know I forgive him completely—and ask for his forgiveness. That part of the process was a surprise to me; forgiving yourself is the most difficult part. You actually do not need the offender's permission. It is all I can do now.

When I learned that lesson, it was time to forgive someone else, my current spiritual man. He had ended our romantic relationship and forgiving him allowed me to accept our new friendship after our breakup. I have progressed to celebrating what he gave me when we were together. Our new connection is not what I originally envisioned, but in some ways it is fulfilling. I rejoice I did not reject his offer of friendship. With my newfound compassion for those whose decisions it was hard to initially accept, I have learned you get more than you give with acceptance.

I guess one of the most important things in life is continuing to evolve and accepting another's offering through compassion. Forgiveness is an important component of spirituality and intertwined with surrender and compassion. Without forgiveness there can be no true love.

To reach this point of forgiveness, I listed my perpetrators' acts that I hadn't forgiven—what had happened, what I had actually lost or suffered as a result and the emotions invoked. When you do this exercise, the magnitude of pain you carry as a result of not forgiving is astounding. Recording it makes it clear. Holding on to these issues produces more discomfort than the forgiveness.

It seems simplistic, but this is the work I did to arrive at this juncture. You must be very honest and kind with yourself during this process.

Forgiveness doesn't excuse bad behavior, but it prevents the anger from destroying your heart. The most important part of forgiveness is to let go of your desire for revenge; it is not productive to want punishment for the perpetrator.

Forgiveness will not happen as a result of the passage of time. It needs to be intentional. With the help of your guides, you lean in on pain to move forward.

You will encounter multiple phases before arriving at forgiveness, acknowledging your grief and overcoming denial. You must accept anger and often betrayal before you surpass it. Many people bargain at this point: "I will forgive, if I receive an apology." This is not beneficial; be magnanimous and do the work forgiveness requires. Surprisingly, you do not need their apology.

Often, if you don't deal directly with rage, it will manifest in depression, a sadness as a result of great loss. You must confront rage, acknowledge it, move through it and surrender to it—a major accomplishment. This process releases you and results in a more benevolent, softer you in a safer place.

Moving forward produces healing that reshapes your life, releasing you from imprisonment. You relinquish pain to receive refuge, comfort and health; you rise as a spiritual soul, which allows you to engage in this forgiveness. Forgiveness is a milestone of spirituality.

Forgiveness to Free Your Soul—the Boat People of Vietnam

It was midspring, and I rose earlier each morning because of the sun's increasing intensity. This time of year, I typically sleep with all the blinds and windows open, even though we still have thirty-degree temperatures; I want to hear the birds at the pond across the street and see the babies in their nest.

But one morning, I did something unusual. For some reason, I turned on the television, which I despise except for Public Broadcasting Service (PBS) stations, and worked mindlessly on washing dishes, making coffee and fixing breakfast.

A story unfolded about Vietnamese refugees. Known as the boat people of Vietnam, they fled their country from the mid-1970s through the 90s—some escaping from prison—following withdrawal of the United States from South Vietnam. It became a huge humanitarian crisis until developed countries eventually accepted these refugees and assumed responsibility for resettling them. I hesitated to allow this television program to intrude upon my placid morning activities, but some words caught my attention. I stopped my domestic chores to listen, and it wasn't long before I was sitting on my couch driven to an activity I hate when I don't understand a language: reading white words on my screen.

The events described from 1988 mesmerized me; I cried through many parts. Horrified, I vicariously experienced the arduous journey of these people, how they left their country of origin, jeopardized the lives of their families and children to embark upon the open sea. They floated toward the coast of China in search of safety, hoping to be rescued by the United States.

The refugees drifted over a month in a cramped craft that was taking on water. It had a malfunctioning motor and no more food on board. The majority of my sadness came from the US military's refusal to assist in saving their lives when they were about to drown adjacent to an American ship on the open seas.

The ship's captain refused to acknowledge the refugees' pleas to receive humanitarian assistance. He gave an order to shake a man from the ladder when he attempted to climb up. The man plunged into the ocean and disappeared. Others risked swimming from their fragile wooden boat to the huge gray vessel and succumbed to the icy waves. No one attempted to rescue them.

I could not comprehend an American captain giving these orders or the officers and crew on board not assisting the refugees.

The story is told from the perspective of Tung Trinh, a survivor. She describes her days on the crowded boat with her child, Lam Than. At one point, Trinh explains how she gave what little liquid she had left to her young child. Then she drank her child's urine. She could only do this once, but somehow it extended their lives. Trinh speaks of how she obliged another woman's request to be held as she died. Though a Buddhist, Trinh talks about the justifiable hate, an intense word, she felt toward those who refused to help her and the other refugees.

About half of the crowded boat's voyagers survived the thirty-seven day ordeal. In the end, with many of the passengers near death, they turned to cannibalism. Trinh resisted at first, but her brother insisted and fed her the meat of a compatriot. She only swallowed, not able to chew the morsels, but it was apparent when watching this film and retelling this story how emotional it was for her.

This Emmy Award-winning movie, *Bolinao 52*, produced by Duc Nguyen, provides an intimate glimpse into refugees' desperate struggles to escape conflict—similar to the experience of recent refugees from Africa and Syria—and seek safety for themselves and their families within our borders.

This documentary follows Trinh and US Navy Chief Petty Officer Bill Cloonan from the USS *Dubuque*. Obeying a superior's order, he refused assistance to the boat people. Cloonan's inability to act significantly affected his life. It infringed on his conscience; he struggled with an immoral decision by his commander and had difficulty accepting his own lack of action.*

The movie culminates with Cloonan's decision to find one of the survivors and confront her about his failure to help. He hopes to relieve his pain and to express remorse. A short time before their meeting, Trinh goes to a fishing village in the Philippines to visit the people who rescued her and the remaining survivors.

---

* The commander of the ship was later court-martialed and stripped of his duties because the military confirmed it is the policy of the United States to assist those in need

At first Trinh is tentative, but then she engages with these people who welcome her with unconditional joy and love. She releases years of pent-up emotion with a celebration of survival. She then meets the American who has traveled across the ocean to challenge his guilt.

He expresses immense pleasure at meeting Trinh and her son and then hesitantly, but bravely, reveals his superior's order that he had no option but to comply with. He expresses the heartfelt sadness that shadowed and negatively influenced his life. Remarkably, Tung recognizes his ravished soul and forgives the man who contributed to her suffering.

They cry for each other's pain. This act of forgiveness washes clean the burden they carried for decades. This story shows how forgiveness can free you from hate and other negative emotions. The act moves you forward in spiritual transformation.

Chapter 7
The Now

There is only one time that is important — now!
It is the most important time because
it is the only time that we have any power.

Leo Tolstoy

I BEGAN MY WRITING FOR *SPIRITUAL QUEST* BY READING A book called *The Power of Now: A Guide to Spiritual Enlightenment* by Eckhart Tolle. At first I felt mad—I was wasting my time reading this book that made no sense in my world. I simply couldn't relate to it; I didn't understand the concept of Tolle's book, thus my frustration.

As I read the book, lots of questions lingered. How do you let go? How do you live in the present? How do energy fields affect us? What are different spiritual practices and how do I identify the ones that work for me, at this time in my life?

Luckily, I did not give up on the book and finally, near the end, found a chapter on relationships—now that I understood.

This part of the book explains how you seldom know someone intimately, how each person might disappoint the other, and ultimately, many relationships unravel. So how do you foster a permanent, deeper affection with someone else? Is it achievable? This part of the book resonated with me and confirmed a statistic that about 50 percent of marriages don't last.

The Now concept is a mixture of Buddhism, mysticism, New Age and Christianity with a bit of Zen blended in to help you remain in the present. Attuning to the Now can serve as an awakening, a shift from an egocentric self to a spiritual being.

Tolle states you must relinquish your ego self, your

sense of being a "me." The focus on *me* often drives you to succeed in the material world, a pursuit that can result in pleasure but not joy. Focusing on success as an end reward keeps you engaged in past and future desires, but living in this very moment has a big payoff—peace and tranquility with a kind of purity.

Some meaningful snippets from my reading include the following:

- You are one with all that is.
- Trust your emotions over your mind.
- Time is an illusion; feel the vibrations of life.
- Everything is alive.
- A shift in consciousness sometimes comes through total surrender in the midst of intense suffering.
- Don't resist negatives—it will compound them.
- Joy and sadness merge into one, which results in peace.
- Nothing real ever dies.
- Acknowledging fear with acceptance will allow you to let go of fear. The right resources and actions will be there when you need them—not before, not after.
- True change from unconsciousness to consciousness happens within, not outside you.
- Each step contains all the other steps as well as the destination—a journey into yourself.
- Listen to silence and create stillness inside you.

When you shift to living in the Now, you will become more aware of your inner body, and this has significant benefits. You slow down your aging process—an eighty-year-old feels twenty inside; you feel lighter, clearer and more alive as your youthful essence shines through. You simply relate more to your inner body age, a timeless zone, rather than your outer body. Your immune system works more efficiently as you self-heal by living in the Now.

You can protect yourself from people's negative thoughts by visualizing a white barrier of light around your body. Negatives and blocked energy can cause emotional turmoil and damage your DNA, leading to inflammatory issues and exhaustion. This blocked energy can be removed daily through a variety of practices such as chakra healing.

You can also do a house cleansing, usually by burning sage (called a smudging) and moving it through all parts of your home with windows closed. Lighting a white candle that signifies light, love and spirit and burning some pine or sandalwood incense increases the effectiveness of the cleansing, as does meditation or prayer. It's also helpful to visualize bad energy leaving.

All objects in the universe are made of energy that vibrates at various frequencies. You can raise the frequency vibrations to achieve positive results through visual and breathing exercises of your energy field.

When living in the Now, your sense of self is not defined by expectations of failure or success because you are not linked to past or future outcomes. This eliminates the need to react to emotions, which often produces fear. Some people see the future as integral to their identity, and they are reluctant to give that up until they see the benefits of the Now, where fear no longer holds them captive. You can uncover the joy, lightness and ease of *being* that flows.

Sometimes it is difficult to stay in the Now, but with practice it becomes easier. It helps to remember a past emergency. During this type of situation, your mind stays in the present; that is why some ordinary people do extraordinary, courageous acts. I have learned this from some of the stories I included in my book *Survival Quest*. For instance, there was a story about how some people survived a bridge collapse and escaped a watery grave by, in part, focusing on the Now.

Tolle's *The Power of Now* is a guide for exploring your higher self, seeking growth and discovering your truths and light. I am thankful I hung in there to complete the book and continue to contemplate these new ideas that shift my perception of how to live daily.

Another important book you might wish to read is *A Course in Miracles* by Helen Schucman, published by The Foundation for Inner Peace. It's a guide to transformation through God and core wisdoms found in most religion. It tackles the validity of evil, sin and guilt, exploring the two systems of perceptions: our ego, beliefs centered around ourselves and limited to our being and knowledge, and our truths, divine wisdom, spirituality, the process of awakening, healing and dismissing the ego.

The cycles in life, the downs and the ups of emotion that accompany failures and successes, last a few hours to a few years. If you do not fail, success becomes empty and meaningless, so you need a mixture of both. Failure is incorporated in every success and success in every failure. Many illnesses arise from fighting feelings of low vitality, but it is part of the cycle needed for rejuvenation.

Strength goes where your attention is; you attract success when you concentrate on the positive. I enjoy creating affirmations and repeating them daily. These are positive statements you chose and speak. As they enter the conscious mind, they also register in the subconscious and can be a power agent for effecting change.

On this journey, you will uncover what assists you in your quest for spiritual enlightenment. One major component is energy; it is helpful to understand the different kinds that affect us.

Energy

Curiosity about the forces from natural settings that have affected my thinking and emotions drew me to explore this subject. With help from my granddaughter, Emma, I uncovered *A Beginner's Guide to Energy Terminology, Energy Fields and Energy Symbols* by Mary Kurus. Here was a child helping her grandma to understand a significant, basic concept of life through her internet research that produced this guide.

Energy plays a major role not only in our body but also in our environment. All objects have this force, even man-made inanimate objects. Most energy forces are based on Eastern cultural teachings from the past, but modern North American and European medicine have recently harnessed these forces for traditional healing.

Energies of the Earth

Earth energies are vortexes of high energy on the earth's grids. This energy also resides in humans, animals, plants, gems, crystals, rocks and man-made objects. Negative energies are created when the energy flow is blocked and becomes toxic, resulting in fatigue, low vitality, confusion, depression and impaired memory.

Plant and flower energy is collected from the sun. Carbon

dioxide and water are processed through photosynthesis, which produces sugars that create energy for animals. Humans feel calm when they are around plants—and plants actually feel. (Researcher Grover Cleveland Backster hooked the leaf of a plant up to a polygraph. When he threatened to cut the leaf, the polygraph needle registered a reaction, perhaps indicating that plants sense human intent and emotion.) Plant and flower energy may be harvested through herbal tinctures. The sun locks in their healing vibrations that, if bottled correctly, can be used later. (To learn more about the curative possibilities of plant and flower energy, please see chapter 2 in my book *Courage Quest* or chapter 10 in this book.) *Tree energy* affects humans in a profound way as they breathe into the universe through their leaves. A tree exhales air-cleansing toxins from the earth. You breathe in its oxygen and then exhale carbon dioxide. The carbon is inhaled by a tree and the cycle continues. Talk to one, listen to its answer and offer it your thanks.

I first encountered tree energy years ago when my friend Al and I visited the Muir Wood National Monument where giant sequoia and redwood trees reach high into the air. Viewing these majestic, peaceful giants, I suggested we hug a tree and give our thanks. Al, not into this kind of thing, surprisingly complied. He put his massive arms around a tree he could only partially encompass and stood there for a long time. It was an emotional experience for both of us for some unknown reason, but in time, I discovered the restorative, life-giving properties of trees.

Rock energy comes from many sources. When at rest, it will have gravitational energy through its mass. There is also energy stored in the chemical bonds of molecules and electrical energy when an electric field is present.

Gravitational potential energy is derived from a possible future event that could release energy, like a rock on a mountaintop that could fall.

I first sensed rock energy one day at Hendy Woods State Park in Northern California. Past the river bridge at the entrance, I got out, smelled the wonderful scent of the newly drenched soil and saw the spring moss explosion. Pink blossoms indicated the trees would soon bear fruit. They would produce the best Grenadine apples, soon to rest in rustic crates with other fruits of the Philo Apple Farm's harvest. I heard, in my new awareness, the gurgling of water as it meandered over rocks below in the Navarro River.

I invited myself to enjoy the moment. I heard crickets and the melodies of multiple birds. I relished a sliver of sun as it cut through the dark rain clouds of the day. I became aware of the energy in the rocks I was laying on by river's edge (see my story on Hendy Woods Campground in chapter 1), not understanding what I felt in these inanimate objects. Acknowledging my newly emerging world of feelings and awareness as I learned to connect to the present.

Vibrations emanate from electromagnetic fields and produce physical movement for all objects in the universe. A lower frequency results in emotions of fear, anger and depression.

Energies of Humankind

Aura is an energy that surrounds, penetrates and extends beyond the physical body with an electromagnetic field. It encompasses humans, animals, plants, and rocks—all objects. Auras have emotional, mental and spiritual layers and they include our souls that live beyond death.

Mind and brain are mental layers of the aura. They connect the personal energy field with the cosmic energy field of the universe. The power of the mind often heals. Mind is the psychic organ attached to the soul and brain and is part of the physical body. Neither the mind nor the brain thinks or knows, so there is no intelligence tapped when using them. They remember, record as a database and operate the mechanics of the body through electrical messages. Alzheimer's disease is a result of a malfunction in this system. Intelligence is accessed when a person's mind calms and is in a receptive mode. The intellect reviews your database of information using logic and determines action.

The unconscious automatically recalls memories of past and present and forms our reaction to situations.

Consciousness analyzes the input garnered from our five senses. Fear is sometimes the result of this process. Consciousness does not create anything; it only studies the inputs and gives you recommendations. Its primary focus is order.

The subconscious is where emotions and feelings exist, stimulated by memory. Depression often results from blocking the overload of emotions. The subconscious views what we imagined as if it was our reality and the same as the experiences that actually occurred creating future memories. Often images of events are recorded through daydreaming.

Superconsciousness possesses infinite intelligence, creative power and lives forever, even after death. It encompasses inspiration, insight and psychic abilities when you allow it to manifest and let go of control. It is our guide. You can ask for answers to issues causing unrest and receive guidance. I learned early on to tap into this powerful energy source.

Energies of the Spiritual World

Chakra is an electromagnetic field that governs the endocrine system, regulating the body's functions including the aging process. There are seven chakras located in various parts of our body through which energy flows.

The *cosmic energy field* connects the earth, planets and stars—the entire cosmos including people, plants and animals. It also links the past, present and future. It is similar to the creator of the universe. It provides us with wisdom, information, insight, balance and intuition.

Healing with intention requires identifying and focusing on what matters to us and pursuing that on a daily basis as we move with our breath and hold positive thoughts in our minds.

Mantras are sounds or words that when repeated affect the physical, emotional, intellectual and spiritual aspects of a person. They are vibrations. The most effective mantras are not verbalized out loud. Mantras are common in organized religion and can often improve one's life.

The meridian system distributes prana (chi, our breath) throughout the body. Acupuncturists use this system to facilitate the healing process.

A *mystic* deals with ancient wisdom, spiritual knowledge beyond our physical and material world. Mystics alter themselves or others by moving through time and space; they have the ability to be in two places at one time. Some believe they heal illness.

Nadis, also known as kundalini, is a yoga term for creative and conscious energies located at the base of the spine. Its psychic abilities channel pranic life energies through the body and are similar to the meridian system.

Negative energies come from negative thoughts you

allow in your mind. The more you think about negative energies, the more influential they become, but you can intentionally turn them into positive feelings. These negative energies move from person to person so you should choose your friends carefully and surround yourself with optimistic people.

Prana, also known as chi and orgone, are nutritive energies of the universe, including all of nature, that you receive through the atmosphere by breathing. It creates holistic healing by strengthening your magnetic field. This stimulates cellular growth, blood flow and healing.

Being *psychic* means accessing clairvoyant energy that encompasses seeing, hearing and knowing to make predictions about people or happenings in the material world. A psychic receives messages from other dimensions.

Spiral energy is an ancient system of spiritual development of continual awareness, energy and alignment with the heart energy that flows in a spiral, like our universe with no beginning and no end.

Spiritual energy nurtures and lifts us beyond the physical. It accounts for our higher feelings that gift us with clarity, courage, compassion, loyalty, faith and love—it is our soul.

Symbols of energy are simplistic shapes found all over the world and through time. Because energy flows through objects, they can be powerful. Circles represent perfection, infinity, the sacred, the divine and the essence of the universe. This shape relaxes us. It is contemplative, encouraging thinking and meditation. The triangle stimulates. Think of the Egyptian pyramids with their high level of energy. It can represent the past or present. You can make a triangle, sit or stand under it and feel its result. A square can represent our material world. There are many more shapes to explore that symbolize and manifest your energy.

To learn more about the major benefits of energy, try this exercise before going to sleep or first thing when you wake up. Focus briefly on your various body parts, feeling the life energy inside each area intensely for fifteen seconds. Then let your attention run through your entire body several times, creating a wave from your feet to your head and then back again. You will feel your body as a single field of energy and identify with the present.

Individual Spiritual Tools

There is so much written on various ways to tap into our individual spirituality that I will only briefly mention some terms and provide a bit of information to get you started with your search.

Crystals are stones have a high vibration that assists in healing. Many cultures have their favorite crystals to effect change. Here is a sampling of these stones and their benefits:

- Abalone: soothes, enhances peace, beauty, compassion and love
- Agate: offers strength, composure and maturity
- Amethyst: promotes, healing, grounding and spirituality
- Aquamarine: clears the mind and balances emotions
- Aventurine: brings luck, abundance and success
- Bloodstone: offers healing
- Clear quartz: enhances focus and purifies energy
- Freshwater pearls: offers healing and prosperity

- Hematite: protects and grounds
- Jade: brings luck
- Jasper: offers healing
- Moonstone: enhances emotional balance and offers healing
- Onyx: absorbs negative energy
- Rose quartz: brings unconditional love and healing to the heart
- Serpentine: brings hormones into balance
- Tiger's Eye: rebalances body, creates optimism and trust
- Turquoise: serves as a master healer and helps with communication

Feng shui is a philosophical way of harmonizing your environment. It originated in China as part of martial arts practice. Today it refers to the force of opposites, female and male energy that influences life.

One tenet of this practice is arranging your life—your home and outdoor space—in a way that brings you peace while rejecting evil spirits. Those who practice feng shui may receive worthy spirits and gather energy rewards from nature. To reap the maximum benefits of this practice, you should purchase a home with inside views of the stars marking the mega constellations governing your birth date. You can find this information by doing a web search about feng shui and marker stars. Doing so will bring positive energy, balance and harmony, into your world and help you to create an uncluttered environment.

With *meditation* you can silence the mind. What is this and how the heck do you do it?

Meditation is looking inward, releasing the to-do lists for the moment and, as they say, just *being*. It is coming to a blank wall that is very relaxing. You live in the present. Meditation reduces stress, allowing you to refresh and replenish your body and mind in a healing way.

There are different approaches to meditating. Breathing meditation helps you to concentrate on your breath. Body meditation allows you to concentrate on your body from head to toe. Loving-kindness meditation fosters positive feelings of adoration and caring for yourself and others. Observing-thought meditation teaches you to notice your thoughts as they arise, label them and then discard each so as not to obsess over them.

Regardless of what kind of meditation you are doing, it is best to first ground yourself. You do this standing or sitting. This process brings your thoughts inward, releases expectations of past and future issues and settles the mind. I visualize my feet in contact with the earth whether I'm on carpet, a wood floor or outdoors. This connection reaches toward the center of the earth as I release my stress and my problems to that core. Then I bring universal energy either from above or below into my body for renewal.

I sit cross-legged with palms facing upward to capture the energy. I close my eyes or concentrate on one point in the distance. I repeat a mantra such as om or anything I desire to halt my normal thoughts. The cool thing is that there is no right or wrong way to meditate. You can do it for five minutes, an hour or longer. No matter how busy our lives are, we all have five minutes to sit and let go of our daily issues, which results in unlimited rewards.

Mindful living is the ability to choose and live your life in this moment. You concentrate on your body, its sensations and the insight it provides. The practice reduces pain, anxiety, depression and improves your thinking and emotional self-awareness. Mindful living helps you to focus on what is real in every moment and provides a clear flow for enjoying the present, before distracting thoughts arise. Actually, you can exist comfortably whether your feelings are pleasant or not. Through practice, one can enter the realm of self-transcendence—overcoming the limits of self to connect with the universe.

With *Pure Thought* the longer you hold a positive thought, the more resilient the energy around you becomes. Pure thought acts as a powerful magnet that draws your desires into a vibrational field, and then all you need to do is respond to the opportunities that arise. If you keep a thought in your mind without being distracted, you have achieved pure thought.

Yoga is a Hindu philosophical and mental practice that uses disciplined poses and postures, breathing and simple meditation. It improves your health and state of mind by relieving stress, increasing serotonin (a healing hormone that assists the immune system and produces a feeling of well-being), improving flexibility, increasing strength, enhancing cardiovascular function, offering weight control, improving your circulation and elevating your consciousness. Your focus increases with an inner harmony.

There are many styles of yoga, here are some of the major ones:

- *Hatha*: uses basic slow movements and breaths
- *Hot yoga*: uses specific poses in heated rooms
- *Vinyasa*: links movement and dance in a fast-paced flow
- *Raji* or *Astanga*: emphasizes self-control, discipline and physical exercises, organized into eight parts

- *Karma*: emphasizes doing what needs to be done, engaging in selfless acts and surrendering to the evolving universe to achieve perfection
- *Restorative*: emphasizes mellow, slow movement for deep relaxation

Living in the Now with Fuchs'

Something was wrong, very wrong.

My eyes were not focusing the way they normally would. I had a premonition; something bad was entering my life. Then a normal yearly exam revealed why. I have a degenerative eye disease called Fuchs' dystrophy. What the heck was this? I found the best ophthalmologist in the country to confirm the diagnosis, and he explained what my future might resemble. He is now my coach. We are now a team.

During our first meeting, I acted like a child when I heard him say, "Yes, you do have Fuchs'." I spewed one hundred questions, interrupting him before I heard each answer. I challenged him with assertions that would prove the verdict null and void. But he steadfastly reiterated the facts about this disease. I would require cornea implants in both eyes at some point; the timeframe and result of the surgery were both unknown. Fuchs' is a fickle disease that moves at its own pace.

Through rebellion, I did not dispel the prognosis. I still have Fuchs'.

Incredibly, I found positive aspects to this scourge having its way with my eyesight. It allows me to daily treasure and honor all I see and to imagine a world without sight, where I will tune into and expand my other senses. It could be a rapid two-year decline or a more forgiving progression taking many years. My concern was, and still is, how much I use the gift of sight for my creative endeavors and activities. During my early teens, I even signed a donor card to pledge my eyes to someone less fortunate when I died. I do not want to lose my sight.

Returning home that day from visiting the doctor, I was numb to the core of my being. I viewed this disruption of my almost perfect life with disbelief, then anger. And finally, I came to where I am today. But at that time I wondered: how dare *it* rob me! I wasn't sure who *it* was, maybe God? My gift to another person now impossible, I angrily ripped up my donor card.

I moved into action to prove my doctor and the world wrong about this diagnosis. I read all I could find on the Internet about this condition, what I might expect going forward (how much pain I would feel, how much clarity I would continue to lose). I also joined a support group. I continued my research, read daily and maintained my contacts for two years as my moroseness grew. The only cure is removing the corneas in separate operations six months apart and replacing them with organs that the body may reject. I would have to take multiple trips to San Francisco for follow-up appointments after both surgeries. Implants are a costly, time-intensive solution that lasts maybe ten years, and then the process would need to be repeated.

After two years of intense worry and time spent researching the disease, one day I woke up and surrendered to the inevitable. I stopped investigating. I stopped looking toward the future and tried to stay in the present. Indulging my fear was not resolving anything. It was only making me sad. I don't control my destiny, so why pretend I could and focus on this disease? I was now able to reset my life and direct it in creative ways with acceptance.

Years later, I sat in the somber doctor's office at the University of California, San Francisco, for yet one more of the sixteen yearly visits to hear the latest report of the Fuchs' progression. The doctor explained I would need surgery in one to two years, but the procedures have improved—the time frame in between implants has lengthened to possibly fifteen years. Unfortunately, I have developed two other eye diseases since the initial diagnosis of Fuchs', which I deal with one day at a time.

I learned from this journey. If you are not in control of effecting a change (which I am not), why struggle with the sadness and the uncertainty of future outcomes? Dealing with these eye diseases has led to major changes in my daily life, but I am blessed to live in the Now where I more easily accept what is, in the present. I live each day as it unfolds, with joy and gratitude for all I have in my life, rather than obsessing over what I could have or might have.

Chapter 8

Love, What Binds and Makes Us Human

Love wasn't put in your heart to stay.
Love isn't love until you give it away.

Michael W. Smith

Love

Love is a priceless gift, much greater than gold.
Love has many stories, too embarrassing to be told.
Love is Cupid saying "Hi."
Love is like a magnitude ninety earthquake in your heart.
Love is warm and cozy inside.
The upside of love can be quite divine.
Love is like a rose just blooming.
Love tastes like a Cutie, so sweet and fruity.
Love looks like a fiery sea of hearts.
Love says, "I need you," every second of the day.
Love sneaks up on you and slaps you with excitement.

Emma (my granddaughter)

WE ARE ALL CAPABLE OF EMOTIONS WE DO NOT EXPECT, even my eleven-year-old granddaughter who is on the verge of exploding into womanhood, is starting to understand love.

Sometimes we are stingy with it; sometimes we are frightened of it. When we release and accept love into our lives, we run the risk of getting hurt, of getting rejected. If brave enough, we risk love again—and it transforms us.

This path of pain, when love fails, creates more longing for joy and connection. An adrenalin rush, love disguised sometimes as lust, welcomes us to risk finding it once again. You may reap rewards for your courage, or not, but for sure, you feel *alive*.

As you mature and learn, you realize love is not just for your benefit—it is to be shared with others. Altruism now encompasses your circle. You assist your fellow man and don't feel cheated when getting nothing in return. Growth has materialized in your being.

This is our introduction to the path of enlightenment. Love enables us to heal past wounds; it reveals life's truths, like success does not bring happiness, and allows us to honor ourselves and others. This is just the beginning of our unlimited love quest.

When I was seven, I developed deep feelings for Paul, the boy next door. It was the first time I'd felt this way for anyone. A range of emotions swirled within me that I somehow translated into love. I'd heard the word *love* before, of course, but was only vaguely capable of defining what it meant. Regardless, I was sure love was a good thing. Yet I definitely didn't understand the heights of elation and troughs of longing and rejection that now intruded upon my childhood. When we were both outside in our respective yards, it excited me when he would turn from his friends and say something to me, usually sarcastic, and then turn back to his buddies for support. But when the other boys were gone, he'd talk nicely to me, even look at me.

What the heck is this? I thought. I knew I liked it and wanted more. I got more.

At twelve, I followed the neighborhood boys around the corner to the back of our clapboard homes as the sun set—no parents watching. We were a group of five—three preteen girls trying to figure it all out and two pretty immature boys with raging hormones.

In our innocence, all we wanted to do was smoke our first cigarettes. Luckily our matches and butts never set our neighborhood on fire. But underlying the experience was a sense of tension we did not yet understand.

I figured it out the next year—pure opposite attraction, yin and yang. Where to explore it? We found a place in our minister's decaying garage behind our property. The building had slits between the lumber siding that let in rays of sunlight—and provided peepholes for anyone who looked closely enough. The minister discovered our nest one day. What we were doing was fairly innocent, but he sternly warned us never to come back or he would tell our parents. The voice of God scarred this teen into improving her behavior for the moment.

Adventuresome, I soon moved on and continued to explore the opposite sex—maybe love, as I framed it. In a terrifying episode during my teen years, I had an encounter with a truck driver. I was walking down the street one afternoon as a driver whistled at my swaying body. I was so flattered that a man in his twenties noticed little ole me. Each day, he drove the same route I used to walk home from school. Soon, I began to wear a scarf on my head; wasn't that sexy? I put on a tighter pair of jeans and waited for that whistle of recognition. I continued this parade until one day he asked me to meet him and go for a ride.

Seldom fearful or worried about taking risks, I joined him in his truck and kissed him until common sense shook me awake (possibly the fear of the minister preaching God's word?). I jumped out of his cab and ran home. I was one lucky girl that something—providence perhaps—intervened on my behalf. More could have happened. I could have been raped, killed or dismembered—my adult imagination abhors what I did as an idiotic teen.

As life went on, I experienced more affection that sometimes resulted in rejection. Self-absorbed, I was on a path to find pleasure and love that surprisingly allowed me to grow into an assertive adult.

Now mature, as they say, I have learned and benefited from that moment with the truck driver, which moved me from my limited, rigid, egocentric outlook to my current spiritual view of life and its abundance.

My definition of love has grown and now encompasses humankind and the universe. Love means practicing compassion and acting on my desire to assist others every day. This path did not take a week, a month or a year to develop. It has taken my lifetime, and it is still evolving.

A 2016 article titled "The 7 Types of Love" in *Psychology Today* defines the multiple types of love. *Romantic Love*—

demonstrated in the stories in this chapter—is often sexual and passionate, defined by the chemistry between two people. Partners often expect unconditional acts (no limits on love's acceptance), similar to parent and child interactions described in *Friendship Love* and *Familial Love*. People are often disappointed when this nurturing, unconditional relationship doesn't materialize.

Friendship Love is a goodwill feeling for a close friend. The story about pallets in chapter 7 is an example of this type of love. It is a bond between those who have common values, interests or activities. It is considered a more emotionally advanced love because it is freely chosen and grows out of compassion.

Familial Love, a type of friendship love, involves strong feelings among family members in an intimate relationship.

Universal Love is what you feel for strangers, nature and our higher spirit—our soul consciousness. It encompasses altruism, which brings an elevated mental and physical high and longevity as you assist those you don't even know. A surprising benefit is that the person on the receiving end of an altruistic act often reciprocates the gift. Altruism seems to open a debt that others seek to pay back—it weaves the fabric that shields, sustains and enriches us. Within universal love, I see hope for world peace.

Uncommitted Love is playful, teasing, fickle, seductive and fun. There are no strings attached. Each person should be self-sufficient, indifferent to pursuing a deeper relationship with the other.

Practical Love is a relationship based on compatibility and shared long-term goals that make the couple committed for various similar reasons and duties. These people coexist in a comfortable emotional space, and they are not focused on cultivating a passionate relationship. Often these are arranged marriages.

And last, *Self-Love* is a healthy infatuation with yourself and encompasses high self-esteem. This important kind of love determines our relationship not only to ourselves but also to others and the world. A person with self-love commits completely to projects and people because they don't fear failure or rejection. They surmount obstacles if they fail, are rejected or experience disappointment. They delight in new opportunities, relationships and risks. They accept and forgive not only themselves but also others.

When talking about love between partners, the ultimate phase is called *Spiritual Love* (not mentioned in the *Psychology Today* article). This kind of love is defined by closeness to a higher being that only comes when two people surrender, find compassion and empathy and conquer their fears to trust each other. Composed of a deep connection with the other's mind and body that rocks your soul, spiritual love makes two people complete. This kind of love resides deep in the soul and allows you to open your heart to others. It brings immense joy and peace. Spirituality and love are entwined, synergistic, each relying on the other. If very blessed, you and a partner blend your two souls, sync together as one. Spiritual love runs deeper than the love you experience at the beginning of a relationship because it now includes your higher spirit. When this type of love is present, your relationship with your partner lasts an eternity. It's always present, even if the person is not. It is a mind-body-spirit connection.

My Loves

When not busy with writing projects, I enjoy traveling across states to visit family and catching up with friends who have become more than that—these are women whom I love. This has come as a surprise to me because I spent much of life caring about and striving to please men. Men, for some unknown reason, were my focus for a long time. Maybe this change was due to desire, a lust for life and human connection, but my spiritual growth has enabled me to now enjoy male and female friendships.

Although I abhor many infringements in my world, I have also learned to accept and love those in my country surroundings, like the wasps who claim my mountain as their turf. They buzz about the cedar tree and house, defying my presence and defending their territory from me. Hey—I paid for these boards, who was here first?

And then, there are the *nasties* as I call them. I guess they are nice swallows, but they attack my blue birds who return each spring to build a nest, mate and lay eggs inside their two-story wooden box. Miraculously, the "house," suspended on a tall pole, has remained for years, despite the harshness of the weather. The birdhouse usually keeps foxes, cats and rodents away from the blue birds' eggs.

Each spring, those majestic blue birds are my welcome to a new season. As they settle in, the swallows attack them, my bird friends who try to keep on keeping on each year in their home.

Why does this happen? Why are there attacks in life? Why can't we respect each other's territory?

Eventually, the swallows succeeded. They drove my pitiful blue birds from their nest, and only two of their four eggs remained. I wondered who got the others—the nasties, the fox or the rodents? I love these blue birds.

Yes, I have loved my entire life to the depths of my soul. And not just wilderness and animals, but I have loved my great woman friends and family as I shed this emotional shield. And men, oh the men in my life. How many have there been?

When I was a teen, someone revealed a statistic. The average woman kisses seventy-two different men in her life. This created a whirl of the absurd as I contemplated if such a number were possible. At the same time, it excited me. I calculated how many boys I had kissed, how many I still needed to kiss and how, just how, I could accomplish this when I realized another earth-shaking statistic: there had only been seven.

Goal-oriented, I now engaged in a mission: finding those guys who wouldn't have a clue as to why they were being kissed. I contemplated the solution at night in bed, while walking to school with my girlfriends, even as the Algebra teacher asked me what pi equals in an equation (answer for all you smarties—ratio of the circumference of a circle to its diameter). She thought I wasn't focusing—but was I ever.

Time was moving on, and my percentages were diminishing. I needed to act *now* and so I started dating to accumulate those kisses. I figured I was beating the odds as I calculated how many kisses I would need to accomplish this goal before I died—seven kisses a year (having forgotten I might be married some day and all this activity would be limited to one man and one qualifying kiss).

Many boys succumbed to my wiles, never understanding my intention. Some became the loves of my life. Mom had never mentioned to me the possibility of multiple commitments when I was younger.

In retrospect, as a mature woman, I now understand how we have many strong relationships in life. There is such a diversity of men, all unique, each offering something that appealed to me depending on where I was in life, what goals and values I had, who I thought I was. I soon learned that love was much more than a kiss. Love is the intimacy of togetherness, the sharing of emotions. I stopped counting the kisses.

I have found wonderful men throughout my life, each one expanding my world as I learned from them. I hope they've benefitted from their time with me as well. Four of the men in my life are exceptional, unique from the others I kissed, so here you will read my story about three sweaters and a hat. In some ways, this story marks my passage into who I have become. I learned to love, get hurt, risk again and experience even deeper feelings that helped me to evolve.

Three Sweaters and a Hat

Three sweaters are neatly stacked in one pile in my closet. They are all men's extra large, but they are different colors and textures. Living in the mountains, I wear them frequently for warmth. People constantly compliment these sweaters, never realizing they are from my ex-lovers, each a unique man in my life. After all these years, none of the sweaters has been sampled by moths while the rest of my clothes are riddled with holes.

I received the first sweater from Carmine, a student of medicine, whom I met while I was studying in the wonderful town of Siena, Italy. Carmine's mother had knitted the sweater for him as a gift when he moved from Bari to Siena. She would probably die or kill him if she ever learned the worst: an American girl in possession of it. What story did he tell her to explain its absence? After all, Italian men are devoted and bound by admiration to their mothers and remain psychologically dependent on them for life.

The sweater is made of flecked gray wool, probably the best his mother could purchase in their southeastern seaport town. She painstakingly sewed two delicate rows of blood-red trim around the cuffs and neck that created a subdued elegance for Carmine, the man who would have a prestigious career.

Wearing a dress and high heels and carrying two suitcases for what I anticipated would be a venture into the unknown, I first arrived in Siena by train. It was 1964, and I was a third-year college student going to live and study in another country through the college's exchange program. I would learn more about life than the course material offered.

My new Italian "family" greeted me — a sister, four years my junior, a mom and dad that seemed very loving. They bestowed multiple kisses on each of my cheeks. I noticed all the dark-haired men, darling and trim, on the periphery, but one handsome man captured my attention.

I didn't understand it at the time, but the men categorized, objectified and rated the newly arriving women, including me. Which male would get which American? We were easier targets for fun than the sheltered females of Italian descent, constantly protected by a father or brothers in this ancient town.

Attending school at the University of Siena, I immersed myself in Italian culture and classes presented in medieval-looking buildings. My professors spoke mostly Italian. In awe, but slightly off balance, I moved ahead sampling all I could find in the Italian culture.

I tried to learn a little Italian before leaving the United States. Some take to foreign languages; however, I was not one of them. But I managed to converse using gestures, and I was an art major, which was more directed to hands-on activities than verbal lessons.

I learned to sculpt, chiseling at unyielding pieces of marble, create frescoes and throw ceramic pots on a wheel. Every day for lunch, I walked two miles over cobblestones flanked with cypress trees through the town center, which was surrounded by a medieval stone wall, to my family's home on the outskirts of town. Lunch included a siesta that everyone partook in before returning to their day.

Carmine, the man I spotted at the train station, was always outside the classroom as I left to walk home. He'd follow me and ask questions in English. Thus, I never needed to learn Italian, and soon we were entwined as an English-speaking twosome. Carmine charmed me and mesmerized me with his compliments. He offered me Baci chocolates as a treat. They had romantic messages inside and were most perfect for our courtship.

To the dismay of my host family, he started picking me up on his Vespa, and I started wearing pants for the ride—a no, no in this ancient town where women only wore dresses. We'd race toward country forests, now our domain, with a treat to enjoy (often an Italian rum cream cake balanced precariously on my lap), and we'd lay down on a blanket—he would feed me a piece of this layered delight, and then I would feed him.

It was a magical period of romance as only Italians can create. He invited me to an elaborate ball for medical students and doctors. I splurged on a lovely gown, a pair of tight black leather gloves and sparkly heels to accent my fairy-tale princess outfit. My old-fashioned family was very upset when they found out I was supposed to meet him at the event; they insisted he pick me up. He showed up on his Vespa, the only vehicle he owned. I could see the displeasure on their faces as I kissed them good night. My creamy yellow dress flowed over the sides of Carmine's matching machine as the wind whirled the silk toward the heavens.

When not with Carmine or attending classes, my days were filled with creating a book of sketches while sitting on Tuscany's flowered hills. I savored delicious culinary treats from the region served by my Italian mother. Some evenings Carmine and I would sample a selection of the finest wines of Italy in the sixteenth-century fortress called the Enoteca Italiana by candlelight. Eventually, I decided the heck with my studies, I could learn later; I was embroiled in a different kind of education—life. Carmine gave me his sweater shortly before I left so that I would always have a part of him near me.

It was difficult to leave my new boyfriend at the end of the semester, but once home I received expensive jewelry from him along with his undying commitment. We would be reunited soon enough; I was planning a trip to introduce my mom to Carmine. However, when my mother and I arrived in Italy, Carmine announced that he had started seeing someone else. It was an embarrassing and expensive lesson. I mourned the end of my romantic encounter thinking I would surely perish, but I survived and became happier than ever.

How do you go from the depth of despair to the height of elation? Maybe it's about growing up and moving on.

My second sweater came from a man I couldn't get

enough of at first. Over the course of twenty-five years, our relationship shifted from love to very close friendship. How many people pull that one off? While dating Ed in my midforties, he bestowed upon me several T-shirts, sweat shirts and, finally, the sweater. It's a dazzling cobalt tweed with speckles of black. The sweater looks good on me. It's spacious, but I don't feel lost in it. When I wear it, it appears I have no hands as the sleeves fall below my knees. It keeps me cozy and reminds me of our worthy friendship that I am honored to enjoy, even today.

I met Ed shortly after my divorce, when I was determined to become the size and shape I'd been in my early twenties. Working out several times a week at an athletic club, I glanced through the window one day and saw him in the adjacent room.

Ed was ordinary looking but had an amazing body, a wonderful smile barely distinguishable under his sexy mustache and a hint of gray in his hair. Was it love? Infatuation? Desire? Why on earth did I have these feelings for him? We had never talked or occupied the same space. I had no idea who he was, what he believed or where he was going in life. But the intense emotion I felt that day, and all the days that followed, could not be quenched.

I soon worked out daily so I could pass by the window and stare at him. I tried not to be obvious, throwing a quick glance and then looking down at my gym bag, maybe bending to tie a sneaker. Anything so he didn't see my obsession.

I didn't think I had made the slightest impression on him. Then one day, it happened! We made eye contact and exchanged some insignificant comments. I almost fainted; I was a schoolgirl with a crush. My face flushed. I could barely reply. I scurried on and then tried to start my workout, which was hopeless as I fixated over his few words and how I'd been so close to him.

We played this game for months. I started going into the weight room where he worked out. Sometimes he was only a few feet from me, and I couldn't concentrate, but I tried. Ready to give up on anything momentous happening after so much time had passed, I felt his hand brush mine one day with his gloved finger. He asked me out to dinner. I accepted, and we began our relationship.

Ed was the most relaxed man I had ever known, the complete opposite of my explosive dad. Nothing in life fazed him. He lived day to day, seemed content with whatever might happen. He required little of me. It was one of the most peaceful times of my life.

Ed and I hung out for a few years while I recovered from my divorce, explored a new perspective on life and confronted an incessant high-tech career with all its demands. He supported me through cancer; I supported him through cancer. I loved him more than my life. We both survived and eventually went our own ways. It was my decision to end our closeness. It was probably the result of needing more time for my daughter and my increasing creative and corporate demands. I was moving forward to a place I didn't understand, or had even known existed, with an accelerated momentum. I was climbing.

When we separated, neither of us cried, but we both felt tremendous regret. He only asked for one thing: "Can you wear red high heels for me?" I am a feminist so no man tells me what to do. But looking back, I realize that wasn't the point of his request. It took me decades to realize I could do that, I would do that, but by then our relationship was no longer the same. The red heels I bought ten years later and never wore no longer mattered. Not giving him what he wanted in that moment was a major mistake I am deeply sorry for. Kind of makes you think about what is important in life — maybe those red heels.

My third sweater, possibly the last sweater gift I will receive, was casually bestowed upon me in my midsixties. Ted was a bit younger than me, like all my men. (I guess I was searching for vibrancy.) A fellow artist in my small town, he was someone I had known for years. A close friend of Ted's had given him the sweater because it didn't fit him. Supposedly too small for Ted's shoulders too — yet one more man in my life with wide shoulders — I became the recipient of a cheerful red-and-black dappled sweater. It was not a heartfelt gift like the other sweaters. But coming from a very private, reserved person, which Ted was, it could have had the same meaning. Then again maybe he just wanted to get rid of the thing. Regardless, I cherish it; it probably suits me the best of all my sweaters. *Why this gift at this time of my life?* I wondered. I now know.

Ted and I met at a photography club, and I felt immediate admiration for the photos of Nepalese woman and children he'd taken on a climb to Mount Everest. My fascination seemed to extend beyond those photos to his persona. His commanding presence and the way he moved caught me off guard. Some thought him arrogant, but his unique, sensitive composure fascinated and attracted me; I wished to learn more. I believe that you should be who you are and flaunt it, which he did. At that very moment of our meeting, in a very public place, I wanted to sit on this lap and put my arms around him — nothing special, just merge with his being.

Years of friendship followed; we even opened an art gallery together. One day, when my current boyfriend and I were at my gallery show with Ted talking to some guests,

I knew. I didn't want my current boyfriend anywhere near me; I wanted to be with Ted. We became a couple on a sunbaked day of lollygagging around his abundant, lush property, our hands that gently connected as we climbed the stairs to his yurt when he said those special words of love. Now in his trap, I gladly submitted to whatever followed.

When we seemed comfortable with each other, he asked, "Do you want me to cut the ponytail?" It hung down to his waist.

"Heck no," I told him." I want you the way you are. I'll never try to change you." From there, our relationship deepened.

We had a very off-the-grid relationship. When Ted first moved to his acreage, he lived in a teepee (not your average digs) and then built a utilitarian yurt up the slope where he lived off the land for several years and fed seeds to the wildlife. Together, we now delighted in the animals' activities, scurrying in and out of our abode. His land of solitude and solace sustained us.

The wooded area had a proliferation of flowers, ferns, prized morel mushrooms in the spring, wild blueberries in late summer, golden circles of aspen rustling in the fall—a simplistic existence, but also a life of abundance. In the coolness of evening, we would rest entwined by the warmth of a fire.

After much research, Ted built an amazing structure, a hay bale house. Soon on site, living and contributing to a unique design of a snail coil that guides you to the shower at its core, I packed a straw-clay circular vesicle to create this shower enclosure.

Ted and I worked on the shower walls as one until he challenged where I was inserting colorful empty bottles in this wall. After all, didn't he ask for my help, my artistic design? It was a challenging moment for us; he saw my independence.

I treasure Ted's spirituality; it has influenced my blossoming awareness as I age. I came to understand the power of simplistic living—only solar for our power needs, water delivered from a well and fresh air to refrigerate our food. I appreciate his desire to live a life of limited subsistence using minimal resources to protect our environment.

Sadly, our world together did not work for a number of reasons. He asked me to leave, and I obliged thinking we could mend the relationship but that never happened. He was—and is—a link to my future, my evolution, but the end of our relationship was something I initially had difficulty accepting.

Ted is the most important lover in my life and gave me the most significant sweater I have received; he has served as my pathfinder—then and now. I respect what we shared and the life lessons he taught me by example: how to live a life of serenity, how to protect our natural world, how to live with compassion, how to give freely to others, how to live simply and spiritually and how to connect with the universe. I believe he was placed in my life, at that particular time, to teach me and assist in my growth so I could eventually support others.

Some people come into our lives and quickly go.
Some people stay for a while and move our souls to dance.
They awaken us to a new understanding;
leave footprints on our hearts,
And we are never, ever the same.

Flavia Weedn

In addition to my sweaters, there is also a hat—a woven mass of straw, a symbol of a man and his life. It seemed to say, "Look at me. I am powerful, defiant—I am me." He *never* took it off, except in bed, occasionally.

The first time I met Michael he was wearing the stylized western hat with a brim that defiantly turned up and down where it wished and an elaborate, flamboyant woven band of adornment; it signified his persona. What to make of that, a man with a hat as an appendage?

In my fifties, Michael exposed me to another side of life—risk and adventure. We constantly played and shared abundant laughter. Well, most experiences were amusing, but the darker aspect of his personality immersed me in despair as I became a partner in his destruction. Our stories are big—too outrageous to tell. We joined as one through our common connection to nature, adventure and risk. This person became an overwhelming attraction to me.

Years passed and *we* are no more—and I am not so judgmental now. I wish the hat and man back into my life.

What alternate direction might have surfaced if we hadn't met? He defined my joy on earth and in the afterlife, but primarily, he exposed me to a world I never knew existed—fearless fun. He honored me by assisting my search for beauty in the world as my sight would soon diminish or be nonexistent because of my eye diseases. He purposely exposed me to the colors of travel, a gift I feel eternal gratitude for. My search for images to remember became *our* search.

What to do with all these wonderful sweaters and the hat? Wear them of course, except the man with the lone hat will never walk the earth again, and the hat is not in my possession. Each sweater has its day, its special memories. Almost perfectly spaced a decade apart, each relationship provided a unique rung on my ladder of development.

When I wear them, no one knows what I feel inside. No one knows that I feel stirred by special men. I guard the sweaters carefully, not wanting any portion of them to leave my being. Maybe I wish they be buried with me.

Three sweaters and one hat, what are they about? Love and growth.

These discoveries are a gift. They stitch the facets of our existence together. They allow us to move forward in a cohesive, beneficial way, to express ourselves as we connect with others, to discover how to expand our spiritual world. Without this connection of love, we are mere flesh, moving through each day without a purpose, possibly without inner joy.

Unfinished Business: What I Did for Love

The phone in hand, a call and then a voice mail prompt, a voice from the past I had waited twenty years to hear again. He was a wonderful pleasure along my path, a very special person who gifted me with an understanding of surrender, laughter and abundant sharing.

I fell for him immediately. Somehow we were on a similar emotional plane during our first meeting in a hardware store. How does it happen in life that two beings can perfectly match? As each word was exchanged, the other grabbed the silence immediately and continued.

We met at Home Depot, our hands grasping a porcelain sink that was on sale. We both hoped to secure it for our individual remodels. I wanted to install it in my home, which I was planning to sell, and he wanted to incorporate it into a renovation of one of his properties.

I watched this interloper who was trying to steal my find. Gray curls were what I first noticed, then his soft eyes, a childish, defiant smile and, well, the rest of him. Immediately I felt love, or certainly lust.

I looked into his eyes. He grasped *my* find tighter—he was not letting go. How dare he challenge a woman in financial need, a woman with a project to complete so she could move on? I had committed to conquering this project on the cheap. Each of us starting to relent, we began a conversation, quipping back and forth, each hoping to win—the conversation and the sink. Looking back, I guess that is what I strove for, to win.

He succeeded—it must have been something he said, or didn't. I don't remember. But actually, I got the prize. He remembered where I worked and traced me down that day. I got a very surprising call at my desk from a man who shopped at Home Depot. He asked if I would meet him "for something," a drink or dinner. In my ecstatic state, the answer, of course, was *yes.*

My first kiss with Al, who was twelve inches taller than me, was soft, passionate and meaningful—even if I did have to stand on my tippy-toes.

We arrived at this relationship from divergent backgrounds. I had a college degree and had been in the corporate world while he had a passion for building projects and acquiring money.

Our relationship began—lavish gifts and conversations. But we ran into a snag. His gray hair had deceived me—I eventually learned that he was eight years my junior. Darn. This was twenty years ago, before we gave women permission to be cougars; the age difference between us was a major obstacle for me. What the heck to do with a gap that wide and a congregational upbringing? We became deeply attached, although hesitant about the age difference. How could it work out in a positive way?

Eventually we were honest with each other. I learned he intensely wanted a child, but I was unable to conceive. At that moment, I realized I would never be able to deliver this gift to the man I adored. In the end, I cared for him enough to let him go, first encouraging and then finally demanding he leave me to find a woman who could fulfill his dream.

Six months after our separation, Al showed up at my house at two o'clock in the morning on New Year's Day. He wore a tuxedo. His tie hung at a defeated angle, and his shirt was disheveled. He looked so attractive yet so sad. Al had left his date and said he wanted me permanently in his life.

For an excruciating year and a half, we broke up and reconnected multiple times. We gave ourselves six months to figure out how to make our relationship work, how to have a child without me giving birth. Joined in pain and frustration, we cried a lot. He kept returning to me to discuss his latest remarkable, unconventional solution to our dilemma, a solution upon which we could never agree.

Finally, we realized the problem was unsolvable. If we adopted, how could I realistically care for a child? I'd be a rickety seventy-two by the time he or she reached adulthood. I eventually insisted he needed to leave me, forever, and get on with his goal. I grieved for years but have never been able release this relationship from my mind and soul.

We were always together in my heart, even when apart. I knew I had to move ahead, become the person I could be, but I had little insight about who that was. I decided to leave my well-paid position at a tech company in California and settle in an isolated mountain town. Since then, I have only worked six months out of sixteen years. Essentially, I "retired" at fifty-five, maybe from all I prized and strove for. I hoped this act of changing my life would surely end the *us*.

There were others I felt deeply for along the way, which helped my pain, but it never dissolved. I was still in love with Al as if I had just seen him yesterday.

Sixteen years after our final breakup, curiosity got the best of me. Was he content or sad? Was he married? Did he have a child? I had to know so I searched the Internet, found his phone number and contemplated if I should call him. I was balanced on my chair at the kitchen counter, rocking back and forth on its spindly iron legs. I debated with myself. Would calling him cause more pain, ignite an almost-sealed wound from years ago?

I finally put my finger to the phone and dialed. Al answered, his voice soft. He sounded surprised to hear me say, "This is Sally. Do you remember me?" At the end of our conversation, I hesitantly suggested we meet to catch up.

He made excuses for each location I suggested. Calling back days later, he told me our meeting would not be appropriate because he was in a long-term relationship that he was thinking about ending but hadn't yet. He said, "Anyway, you need a mountain man." He is definitely a city fellow. He loves cars, cell phones and the hectic pace of a city environment. We had become opposites (or possibly always were)—not what I envisioned when we first met. We didn't speak again. I did not know the path his life took and he did not know mine.

Four years later, during a burst of energy and focus for some unknown reason, I committed to downsizing my possessions once again—and my world changed. Happy with my existence and feeling blessed, I opened a drawer and found a white envelope. Inside was a stack of glossy photos of Al and his first remodeling project that I helped him with.

Why had I kept them? I hadn't looked at them in years and they were taking up space in my life. The more salient question was what to do with these photos now? I wouldn't contact Al and be rejected a second time. His message was very clear—we would never be again.

I remembered my mother's advice when Al and I had first broken up. "Leave him alone," she'd said emphatically, with fondness for Al. And I had left him alone. Unlike me, she is a sage, not driven by emotion and passion. I contemplated what to do about the photos. I should just drop the envelope of memories into the shiny metal can and be done with it, but I couldn't release the envelope from my fingers.

Finally, a force moved me to the computer once more to uncover his old business address. Might he still be at that location? I decided to take a chance because these images provided a snapshot of an important time in his life, a remembrance of his first successful construction project. I knew he would value them. I enclosed a short note about my life, wished him well and attached my business card. I had zero expectations of a reply.

Days passed. Upon returning from a camping trip, I found that envelope tucked in my mail. It was marked *Return to sender*. Was he annoyed with me? Why wouldn't he accept it? Then I looked closer and saw the reason: *No such person at this address*. Apparently, he no longer occupied that office.

Now I was fully invested in my mission—get those

photos out of my life and into someone else's. I never give up until a task is complete, so I decided to call him. Back to the computer I went. I grew frustrated because I couldn't find a phone number or maybe I didn't try hard enough. I sat in my comfortable chair looking out at the mountains and asked the universe for guidance.

Something compelled me to find an address book buried in my closet that I hadn't glanced at for years. Neatly written next to Al's name was a phone number. This would be my final attempt to get the photos to him. If it didn't work, I would dump them in the smelly green trash can outside.

This time I didn't hesitate on the phone; I was ready for a conclusion to these efforts. The call went to voicemail, but it was one of those automated recordings—I didn't know if I had actually reached Al. I left a brief message about the envelope and asked if I should mail it again. If so, I needed his address. Then I hung up.

Ten minutes later my phone rang, and all I heard when I picked up was "Al." Initially, just that. It was him! We talked briefly as my heart pounded almost out of my chest and he gave me the address to mail the photos. I mentioned I was packing for a trip to California, so I couldn't talk. He suggested we meet during my visit and said three times that he was excited to see me and would disclose a recent life-changing event.

I told him I would let him know when I had free time during my travels. Was this a smart thing to do? Probably not, but I wanted to learn about the event. I needed to know. *Oh, please don't let him have cancer or some grave illness*, I thought. Then other possibilities assaulted my thoughts: Had he married? Had he fathered a child (in or out of wedlock)? Had he found religion? Become gay?

I found some time to see Al during the last portion of my trip. I was visiting Mom, and she always took a nap in the afternoon, leaving me time to run some errands—or have a quick lunch with Al. It would be convenient and in my neck of the woods. I left a message with my proposal and expected to hear from him in precisely ten minutes. I knew his pattern now.

Wrong. He didn't call for ten excruciating days. In the interim, I said a swear word about men and decided to write him off, thinking maybe it was for the best. When Al finally got around to calling, he suggested we meet in *his* area the day I was leaving California, for a two – to three-hour lunch. It was inconvenient—during peak traffic time, I would have to negotiate the gnarled San Francisco roads to Sacramento where my night's stop would be a turn-of-the-century hostel, but I agreed.

When I disclosed all this to my mom and my sister, they also wanted to know about his "event." Now everyone was onboard to hear the answer, even Mom's caregiver. I needed to meet him. My sister suggested I buy a new blouse. *That's ridiculous*, I thought. *I am me, who wouldn't accept Sally in a secondhand T-shirt?* In retrospect, it was worth the bucks.

Driving to our rendezvous, I couldn't find the freeway exit MapQuest had routed me toward. I accidentally arrived in a bad part of town. What to do? The only person I saw was a very unusual-looking lady walking down a street of dilapidated buildings. She had straggly brass-orange hair and wore very short shorts, high heels and a leopard-print shawl draped over her shoulders. (It was ninety degrees outside.) As I got closer, it appeared she might be a *he* in drag. In desperate need of directions and seeing no other option, I abruptly stopped, jumped out of the car and asked her for directions to the restaurant where I was supposed to meet Al.

Definitely from another world than mine, she moved close to me, very close. I smelled her whisky breath. I sensed she might pull a knife and stab me. After so many years of dangerous journeys, I didn't hesitate to listen to my intuition. But nothing happened. Silent, possibly a bit incoherent at the moment, she just pointed to where I should turn at the next corner. I rapidly got back in my car and locked the doors. Again, a swear word for Al.

Finally, I made it to the restaurant—unusually early—and waited in the parking lot. I intended to make a grand entrance wearing my new, partially see-through top and brown lace bra barely showing underneath. Tight black stretch pants and some flashy jewelry I had never worn during our time together completed my ensemble. I had even styled my hair. I was ready. Maybe I looked like a second hooker on the route, but *I wanted to hook this man.*

A phone call. Al explained he didn't expect me to be at the restaurant at our appointed time—he would be late. I emphasized I was *there* and he was not. He floundered for words. I desperately said, "So, you won't be coming"?

"No, I'll see you."

My heart sunk—he meant someday. I asked him if he was ill. "No, I'll be there in thirty minutes," he said.

I got us a table and waited, uttering yet one more curse word and thinking I had used my quota for the year. I seldom say those words. While I was staring at my phone, a presence became apparent. A man stood adjacent to where I was sitting. I looked up. At first, I contemplated who this could be. Who was interrupting me as I waited for my long-lost love? Then he smiled, he spoke and I knew.

Al sat down across from me. He looked multiple decades older (Well, we both were.), his sparkle and laughter gone. We launched into a two-hour conversation, similar to the give and take we'd had before. It was as if no time had passed. We were each anxious to hear about the other's life, but for now, he wanted to know all about mine.

When he was satisfied, he said, "Now, my news. I recently experienced five heart attacks and a stroke. With twelve stints in place, they can't do heart surgery. There is no cure and I am on multiple medications."

I felt devastated for Al and his future. His boyish grin, his curly hair, his god-like build were all gone; he was now very lean and very bald. I kept starring at him trying to uncover the man I knew from the past. I searched deeper and deeper into his eyes to find an inkling of this man I had expected and wanted to find. I wished he would come back. But, with time, during our conversation, a bit of familiarity surfaced, and that was enough to hope I'd see him again.

When leaving, he asked me about where I lived and suggested he might visit Idaho someday. He wanted to know how many people lived in my small town and expressed concern for all the rednecks running around with guns and killing animals. I agreed with some of that, but I also told him I lived in a state with wonderful people and striking scenery. Silence. I offered to pick him up at the Boise airport, told him he could stay in my guest room on a floor separate from mine, carefully suggesting the type of visit. Again silence.

I asked if he wanted a copy of my book *Survival Quest*, which I was pitching on that trip. He said yes. I then asked him to read the story about Ed. He knew Ed, but not that he had been hospitalized for a heart attack, had fallen into a coma for two months and then had miraculously recovered. It might give him hope.

"Do you read books?" I asked, knowing the answer.

"No, but I will read this one and call you after."

With a quick parting kiss, I got in my car and sped into a tangle of metal moving through the city, which I hate. During the drive home, I had time to think. It was all about this man. Would he actually call? I made a pact with myself not to call him again. What did I want to do with this relationship?

Maybe I should have said something different, acted different, but at that moment, I didn't know. I drove thirty minutes north realizing as I moved ahead in life, it simply didn't matter if he wasn't a part of it.

A very different twist from what I had expected after giving him up for all the right reasons at the time. He hadn't married or had a child. I realize now at seventy-two, with my active lifestyle, I certainly could have raised a child. Looking back, was it worth demanding that he leave me?

My life moved in amazing directions after we broke up. I left my high-tech, high-stress existence to find tranquility and beauty here in my chosen state. I traveled as I had always wished throughout the world, found my true self and became a photographer and author to inspire others' lives.

What might have I experienced with Al in the city? Possibly we would have adopted a child—that would have been exciting and fulfilling. I'd always coveted another. If we were still together, I would live daily with a man I am confident would honor and support me emotionally. It would be a very different type of adventure than what I have experienced. Could I be satisfied today? Could he?

Before meeting Al in that restaurant in California, my daughter cautioned me not to go. "You can't go back in time, Mom," she'd said. I explained my reason for seeing him. It wasn't that I wanted to go back in time. We had never completed our time together, and now I needed to know if our relationship would resume or conclude. I suppose you could say I needed closure. If we were together now, I would reap love and have a tamer life — maybe I am ready for that as I age and have accomplished all I wish.

But it comes down to this. I would never leave my town and state. My essence is here and I can't relinquish it. I could visit him and he me. Would he want that? Would we fall in love again, enough to give up our current paths? Realistically... no. But I have thrown this thing up to the universe that is in charge of my future anyway. So, thankfully, I don't have to make a decision. Our paths have already been decided and will become apparent soon enough.

Love requires risk, as I always say. We might get hurt, but the glory of our soul surfaces from these intimate relationships; it is worth that step forward. Maybe I've loved too little, maybe too much. I am relatively sure I have erred on the latter, and that is not a bad thing.

The Pallet World

Friends are those rare people who ask how we are and then wait to hear the answer.

Attributed to Ed Cunningham

Friendship is so special; it provides a warm feeling of support. When you ask a real friend for something, you know this person will follow through—even if it is inconvenient—with a smile. My friends have been there to listen, advise if need be, motivate and wipe away my tears. One friend I had not seen in months responded immediately to help when my plumbing backed up and overflowed into my tub. It was snowing outside, and he was barely able to navigate my unplowed driveway, but together we solved the issue. That's a friend.

You never know what changes your world, even in a minor way. Maybe a friend.

One day I was looking out at the new spring colors through the polycarbonate clear panels on my sun porch. The vibrant green sprouting grass swayed side to side in the afternoon breeze. (I always have a breeze because I live at the top of a hill with few trees surrounding my home.) The grass was a bit deformed looking through the plastic but still attractive.

This simple, utilitarian room enclosing my firewood took shape as a gift from my friend Ted. I decorated this room as a celebration of life with my special art, stones and feathers that I had collected from my trips, along with a forty-dollar secondhand Persian rug. I accented the room with plants that others had generously given me, chimes from my daughter that sing wind spirit songs and other keepsakes that provided comfort. Now, it was the perfect place to retreat to at the end of the day.

With delight, I dusted off the cobwebs from the table my great-grandpa had built to celebrate his son's marriage. The table's legs fold up so it can be used for camping. The surface is a faded burgundy, but glimpses of green, a color added circa 1940, peek through. Each color struggles to dominate. Previous generations covered most of the original wood, many times, and the paint has chipped through years of use and neglect so it is quite an ensemble of color. Even though it sat in my garage for years, providing a home for spiders to spin their webs, it is a piece of my family and one of my favorite possessions; I welcomed it into the new room where I enjoy my simple pleasures.

I glanced at the north sky from my patio and then at neatly piled stacks of wood rounds ready to burn. I respect wood and occasionally—well, often I admit—can't part with many pieces. Instead of letting fire consume them, I have set many aside. I've been doing this for years and now have quite a collection of rounds that qualifies for my "save pile." Save for what? Well, now there is a use for this log, so I gingerly positioned it in the right place for a footstool.

I roamed around the cluttered garage. A friend has suggested that I keep too much junk. I see treasures I can't let go of. And, voilà, there is another item I can't part with—a brass chandelier, probably from India, each wire cut from its original use to provide electrical lighting. It is useless to anyone but me, and, yes, it is also covered in cobwebs. This ornate piece, with absolutely no value or utilitarian purpose, is perfect for my purposeless room.

As abundant light streams into my new space, I realize the benefits of solar and what it might do for my plants, considering there is less warmth in the Northwest. Now because of this protected room with an expanse of clear panels, I started buying the varieties of vegetation I had always coveted but could never keep alive. It became a greenhouse.

I gathered the magazines I never read, the candles I also lacked time to enjoy and began sitting in this room, all the while weaving together a collage of wonderful possibilities in my mind. Sometimes I turned on Bach or rock music inside the house, depending on my mood, opened the door and dreamed. I rarely took time for me with no objective or goal in mind. This felt amazing. And that is also what got me into my predicament.

There's a patio on the north side of my house, but I never seemed to find the time to enjoy it. In fact, Ms. Queen of the Patios had a front, back and side one. I seldom used any of these. Sitting in my sunroom and looking outside, I contemplated building another patio a few steps away where I could enjoy morning coffee, sit outside to see the foliage dance and smell its aromas while watch the birds fly overhead and sing their songs—assimilate with nature.

Was it a huge mistake to build one last patio (and I do say *last* because there were no other places left to construct one)? Was it worth it for just one person?

Let me tell you what happens when you start dreaming. I told Ted that I wanted to find a wooden pallet or two and bring them to my property. It would be an inexpensive way to put a simple table outside; after all, there is a cheap collapsible plastic one in the garage that would work (also cobwebbed). I reasoned I'd discard the pallets when I got over this patio thing.

Ted called the next day. He had found pallets at a lumberyard—and they were *free*. Oh, my favorite word. How could I turn them down? But his vision was much different than mine. He said we'd need to get six because, as he described it, two would be small for a table and chairs. No, I argued, two pallets would be enough for my plastic table. Well, he created doubt in my mind and I succumbed. We returned home with six pallets that would make a seven-by-twelve-foot rectangle.

First, he said, we'd need to put down plastic to kill the

weeds. He also wanted to level the soil—oh no, I stood my ground on this one. We would need a plow or a very strong person and I had no budget for this with my *free* project.

To make the surface and tie the pallets together we would need additional wood. It was out of the question to purchase. He moved a trashcan to make space for our endeavor, and asked, "What's in here?"

"Oh, the extra flooring I installed in my house," I said. So now the elegant, hand-scraped cherry wood hanging out by my garage would soon cover my pallets. I wondered how the cherry felt lowering itself to pallet status.

I did not have enough wood so I patched the uncompleted surface with other scrap wood that hung out in my garage. We whipped it together in a day, stood back and looked at the uneven structure. It rested on unleveled soil and there were gaps at the ends where pieces of wood weren't long enough—what a mess, but in my eyes, perfect. I was delighted. I enjoyed the eccentric things in life, and between the platform and patio projects I started to move out items in my garage.

Now I had to stain the wood—quickly because it would soon rain. Exhausted and suddenly horrified, I sat on my rocking chair. What had I done? Why had I done it? I had built something I did not need and might never use. Worse, how the heck could I ever get rid of this structure now that it had blossomed from two simple pallets into *this*?

It must serve a purpose. I wasn't sure what that might be, but I was convinced it would come to me. It had to be a place I wanted to hang out. It needed to be filled with my treasures. Right now it was a bare "floor," if you could call it that, staring at me.

It required a wooden table, not the plastic table I had originally had in mind. Focused, I took a few hours and searched my unpretentious town of few options. My book deadline loomed in two weeks, so I had little extra time to play decorator with a bare floor, but I hate unfinished projects.

Luck, maybe, helped me unearth a colonial table (I abhor colonial) with yucky curved legs and a crack through the top of the wood. I bargained—who else could she sell it to? It was useless I told her and closed the deal for thirty-five dollars. I wondered how I would fix this thing.

My "helpful" friend said he would assist in transforming it into a solid surface. I bought metal bars to put underneath the table, and he shook his head. "There is only one way," he said. "We rip it"—cut it I learned—"down the middle to make two pieces." Then he suggested we put those cute little wood oval plugs in to join the sides, glue and clamp."

A sinking "*Oh*" was my reply. More work, more time, but no more money. He made me do much of the work to learn wood construction. Was that what I had signed up for?

Now there was glue on the tabletop as well as my Maui shirt I cherished from the 70s. When the glue dried, I needed to sand and refinish the wood, no solution for my shirt. Additional work.

While I waited a couple days for the next phase of the table refinishing, I searched for outdoor rugs to put under it. I was now feeling attached to that table, which would soon emerge to decorate my new patio. The rug was not cheap, but it was necessary to hide, kind of, the uneven wood floor we had installed.

I saw the absurdity of all this. Now, all I needed to do was recite my list, hoping by saying it out loud it would magically disappear into the ether and I would be done:

- Put a second coat of stain on the patio.
- Find a tiny piece of molding to complete the perimeter (because I had misjudged its length when cutting).
- Assemble the table and decide if glue would hold our cuts together or if they needed to be reinforced. (I purchased those metal strips for some reason that might be apparent soon.)
- Finish the tabletop (stain or paint—paint definitely sounds easier).
- Decide how to erect a shade area. (I realized the deck got too hot in the afternoon sun.) I also need to consider the near hurricane-force winds that blow through my property most afternoons.
- Learn how to build a short fence on one side—cheap—that could withstand the wind and be disassembled in the winter to protect it from roof snowfall. Thinking lattice but that would need posts and how the heck could I dig holes for them with my rotator cuff issue? Finally, how could I remove them when the snow flies?
- Figure out how to control the pesky hornets who think the sunroom and vicinity is theirs. When I shoo them outside they interfere with my work, and they get more aggressive each day. (Didn't mean to invade your space, please don't sting me.) Each year is progressively worse and I am told they live in the pine and cedar trees I have struggled to plant each year on my almost tree-less property, or even worse, the wood stored in my patio.
- Decorate with potted plants, maybe flowering trees that will discourage hornets, but how to secure them in the wind?

- Create a serving counter or cabinet to keep items handy for dinner or work, but how to protect it from the rain and wind?
- Figure out how to shield that table that I bought, have spent hours fixing, and am intensely attached to from the rain?

Humbled by this process, I now had little time left to complete my book. Had I asked for too much when I possessed so much? What on earth did I actually want? Probably not a pallet wood patio.

I know the universe and my angels always deliver the answers that are inside of me, if I listen, slow down and stop moving in frantic action. I did learn from this project that was inspired by my daydreaming. I never need more material possessions, but this relatively inexpensive venture allowed me and Ted to collaborate on a project that, upon completion, provided a sense of fulfillment. It encouraged me to relax and enjoy life, stop my constant striving after goals and savor hidden treasures. That's not a bad thing.

A special friend is a guide, a special friend is an enabler of what you wish, but maybe, just maybe, do not always tell them your dream of building a patio. When you listen with your heart, instead of your head, your outlook on life changes. You feel instead of think. With this, you move into a deeper understanding of life with warmth, compassion and adventure; sometimes it's a bit more effort but so worth it.

Chapter 9
Fear

*Fear defeats more people than
any other one thing in the world.*

Ralph Waldo Emerson

Flying as a bird

All of us have this wrenching emotion that is difficult to surmount. Fear can actually bury you, but it becomes necessary to overcome and extinguish obstacles to move ahead in life. I wrote extensively in my first book, *Courage Quest*, about fear as part of my mission to confront and overcome. Traveling solo to challenge developing country destinations was my solution. The spiritual world offered this tool to help me accomplish my goal. It was a suggestion I could not ignore.

I continued in this direction, until my family suspected I was crazy with all the risking. It didn't matter; I had to. Now I understand. It allowed me to harness my higher power. Go figure. You need to trek on your individual path to discover how best to confront fear and overcome it. In my fifties and sixties conquering fear became my initiation and entry to maturity. Through this journey, I discovered I had courage, strength and power.

First and Only Sky Walk

When I review all the wild and dangerous challenges in my life, I quickly grasp the one I most feared. There is no turning back when you are twelve thousand feet in the clear blue with a downward trajectory and dependent on your equipment and guide for your life.

When my niece, Kate, turned eighteen, she decided to

celebrate by going skydiving. I still have not learned her reason for picking such an extreme activity, but possibly it was a discussion Kate and I had when she was sixteen and she asked, "Is there anything you never accomplished or wished to do in your life?"

"Yes, skydiving," I said assertively.

Once I desire something, it never leaves my subconscious until completed, and skydiving had been an unfulfilled, tantalizing but fleeting wish for thirty years. I strive to challenge myself, embark on journeys where few go, so I came clean when she asked. Apparently, she did not forget that answer, thus her phone call right before her eighteenth birthday. She proposed this as an activity we'd enjoy together. Enjoy? I attempted to be positive and enthusiastic.

"Wouldn't it be perfect if you and I do this together?" she asked. I concluded it would be a first for both of us, an event we would always remember. It could prove an adventure for each of us, in different ways.

"Of course it would be amazing to do that with you," I responded. After all, what would she think of Aunt Sally (someone who lived bravely), if I did not accompany her? In my mind, I still saw her as the cheerful baby I once held in my arms. How could she be so grown as to suggest risking her life doing this activity—or had she considered that? It was clear she would need me on this exploit.

I was elated when Kate hung up, but my body tensed as I started thinking about what I had committed to—its challenges, risks and possibly deadly outcome. A girl of action, she soon booked the trip and even arranged for celebratory glasses of champagne when we landed.

The night before the jump was very uncomfortable. Nightmares intruded on my sleep. Excuses soon formed in my mind for why I couldn't do this. They ranged from the reasonable (*At fifty years old, I have high blood pressure, a bad back. You would have a better time without Auntie*), to the sublime and ridiculous (*Maybe I'll throw up and croak choking. Maybe I will collide with a blackbird in the sky and kill both of us in midair*).

Maybe . . . I didn't have the guts to do this.

The word *courage* convinced me I must go. Besides, one of my greatest wishes would be achieved; I would fly for the first time in the heavens, free as a bird.

Kate and I met in Hollister, California, at the skydiving field where we were required to watch a film about what to do on our flight and what can go wrong. Then we signed tons of disclosure and release papers. My stomach started to acknowledge it didn't want to participate in this sport.

After suiting up, the two of us walked across the tarmac. My legs started to shake. Our joking jubilation stopped, and it was a stark promenade to the airplane, our silver ship of destiny. Both of us in silent contemplation, Kate and I moved forward.

We boarded and sat down on the frigid steel benches, the people who would be tethered to us, our life support, sitting behind. Could I bolt? They had not closed the door yet. But suddenly the metal door was slammed shut, barring any defiant move to the world beyond. The propellers began whirring and soon there was lift off.

Our pilot was feeling generous. He took us up an additional four thousand feet, to twelve thousand instead of the usual eight they boast is the highest skydiving in California. *Thanks a lot, Pilot.*

The door opened to the heavens. I studied the window to the blue, punctuated with a few puffy clouds floating by. Yes, we were in the air, high in the air as I acknowledged my instructor's click, a link to my belt. Will that hold? How securely is it attached? How sturdy is the strap material connecting the new us?

Sure I'd throw up — fear had settled into my body. Only at this juncture, before I left the confines of the metal enclosure for the spacious sky, did the true meaning of my commitment to my niece, along with the possible severe consequences, resonate inside of me. My mind was filled with what-ifs. My previous life flashed before me like a movie from the past, and my future became grim with the possibility of a failed landing. We dove into nothingness as we exited our plane in a somersault, our arms reaching outward as birds in flight.

Once out of the plane, every portion of my mind and body focused on the free fall. My memories left. I had no future concerns. There was only the Now — a present moment of joy. Amazing joy.

The air filled my lungs; maybe a bit too much, and I was barely able to breathe. Soon the force of the wind dissolved my cheeks into sharp angled bone, deflating my body. I will never forget the clear, intense blue of the atmosphere, the curvature of the earth I viewed below, the colors and patterned fields of green beauty.

Eventually objects enlarged, and whoop — there was the snapping sound of the parachute inflating. I was reluctant to return to earth. I had a passionate desire to slow down, suspend our fall. But it was not to be. We bounced when hitting the drop zone of the field. It was sad to return to where humans belong, but my spirit was jubilant as I celebrated one of my most memorable journeys.

I will always feel extreme closeness to my niece who allowed me to fly. We bonded on that fall to earth; I am sure our lives will never be the same. We gifted the meaning of courage to each other.

Luckily, I learned through committing to this dive. Once I left the plane, nothing mattered but the flying, the glory of freely soaring. This act, with a risk of death, exposed me to the *Now*.

When you conquer fear, you receive enormous benefits. Each accomplishment results in internal growth and accumulates into a body of confidence. At that time, I did not consider the transformation, but now I have learned—this is one reward of living in the moment.

Was this experience Kate's attempt to complete my goal or hers? I could have saved myself much discomfort the day preceding the dive if I had practiced living in the *Now*. Love to you Kate.

Courage Conquers Fear

In the book *The Fear Cure* by Lissa Rankin, MD, she discusses how fear is panic—accompanied by anxiety—that results from a perception you are unable to control your life. It weakens your immune system making you more susceptible to illness, but there are so many other consequences.

Fear undermines your safety and security and the willingness of others to offer acceptance. This is major as it plays with your mind. Fear blocks your integrity, your ability to be your true self. You wonder what others may think about you. You may question whether you are good enough. It slows your progression toward destiny.

When you find strength—the key to conquering fear—others may feel uncertain about the new control you exhibit over life. You may temporarily lose the support of those close to you. They may feel confused about your new actions, the different person you are becoming. Your relationships with them may become unstable.

But this newfound courage allows you to start attracting others who are also exploring their higher consciousness. They are drawn to the light and power inside you that illuminates.

Surrender is a simple but scary process. Part of this submission is relinquishing fear. You offer up what is not working in your life to the universe, your desires, your fears, your need to control. You must learn to trust your internal self, and the universe, to protect you and guide you to solutions. You "courage" through it.

The universe gives joy, unconditional security, support, physical and professional wellness and a sense of connection to the divine. What results is that you bond with your inner self and gain freedom.

You can face and overcome your fears today, one step at a time. A courageous person knows they can do something, is prepared to engage and moves ahead despite the fear. Each success will compound as you overcome. Success builds success.

Destinations with the Journey in Mind

My first solo backpack trip required a surge of courage drawn from deep within. I cleaved to what I never suspected I possessed—a spirit imbedded in me, not tapped to this extent until this journey. I learned to hone my survival skills during my trip to Kenya and Tanzania.

Despite the warnings about abduction, mayhem,

robbery and rape in this part of the world, I tentatively decided to go anyway. As a single woman striking out alone to conquer her fears, I learned from my adventure travels. I always strived to challenge myself, veering off the normal treks. I have lived a very full life with close relationships, variety in my work, creativity, numerous wanderings and an excellent support system.

Through the years of going beyond the norm, I learned how to handle difficult situations. I'd step back from my emotions, analyze the problem, review possible solutions, visualize the outcome and discern how I would act. Often I experienced positive outcomes, which built my confidence and dissolved fear.

Prior to these trips, I had one of my first confrontations with fear and courage. The day after my college graduation I ventured across the country in my Volkswagen, paper bags in my car filled with the basics to start a new life in California. I split expenses with a stranger from my hometown. Left with little money and on my own, I arrived in my new world of Hollywood, California. I was scared.

I chose this town when I saw the huge welcome letters spelling out the only recognizable name I knew in the West—currently a foreign land to me. Cars whizzed by on the freeway. My heart pounded. I didn't know which exit to take or if I was moving north or south.

Possibly, just possibly, I had been too impulsive, taking off on a whim the day after graduation with no destination in mind. Driven by the normalcy, monotony, the lack of opportunity in Buffalo, New York, and a relationship that had no passion, I had to leave.

The hardest was saying good-bye to Mom and Dad. They had been my lifeline for the past twenty-one years. I would miss them, but worst of all, I supposed they would grieve the loss of their firstborn and I had to take ownership for that. As with most significant life changes, something pushed me forward though I had done little detailed planning. I would not lose my course, bolt in fear and ignore the new path that had presented itself.

Once in California, I dropped off my new companion of five days. We had shared the cheapest of cheap, not always safe, accommodations across the country. How would I survive on pennies—$150 to be exact? I pulled off an exit and aimed at the familiar word "Hollywood."

I stopped at a dilapidated building with a neon sign from yesteryear blinking "Dinner." A lady in her mid-forties with hair piled atop her head and a calico apron circling her waist lead me to a booth. It had torn plastic seats and a jukebox and was set with chipped ceramic plates. I ordered a bowl of tomato soup—"Oh, and please bring some extra crackers and *lots* of butter." I would live on tomato soup, crackers and butter for the next week.

I was starving that first night as reality set in, along with fear. Truly alone, I had little money or even a place to stay. Night was approaching—this wasn't good. I had to conserve the meager amount of cash I had; I couldn't afford a motel, but I must settle somewhere for the night. Fear turned into focus.

Driving around, I saw a crumbling dusty orange brick building surrounded with defeated trees that had long ago dropped most of their parched branches in defiance of neglect. A loosely painted sign posted above the grimy door read "Men's Home." Well, I wasn't a man, but I did require a "home" and it looked cheap—only six dollars a night for a transient flophouse. Somehow, I convinced the manager that I needed a place for a few nights until I got settled in the city of glitz and glamour.

I parked in the dark, trash-laden underground garage and took a load of bags up to my second floor room. It definitely was not the Ritz. From the hall, I could view the small accommodations through the missing wood on the door. Inside I saw a paint-chipped metal headboard, one side table and a chest with drawers slouching at various angles.

At that moment I gave up any hope the furniture might store my clothes without collapsing to the heavily stained, worn plank floor. Inside, a peeling silver mirror hanging precariously from a skinny nail reflected the image of a frightened, exhausted transplant. I barely recognized myself. Perhaps once it had been an attractive mirror, but the faded gilt frame had almost been destroyed from years of use and abuse.

I lowered my bags to the floor and walked down the creaking steps to secure my next load of possessions. In the dank garage, a black man approached. I could barely make out his silhouette due to his color and the lack of lighting. My heart raced. I quickly formulated an escape route, and if need be, a plan to defend myself. (I had learned some self-defense techniques during a course in college.) I would use brute force (sure) to disable my attacker.

He approached me, his unshaved face very close to mine as I sweated in terror. I was definitely not in control and would soon flee, but then he smiled and in a singsong tone asked if he could help with my move.

Could it be a trick to abscond with my precious bagged items? No, I doubted they appeared precious to anyone but me as I pulled the paper closer to my body. Maybe he was trying to direct me to a less safe corner of the lot to attack me. No, I thought, I am gifted at reading people and their body language. Maybe he actually intended to help. I learned true survivors listen to their intuition throughout life.

At this point in my life, I'd only known one person of color and that was at my university. I had grown up in a white neighborhood where racism was common, so trusting this man was a stretch for me. But I took a chance and let him help me, thinking risk = reward. I was truly exhausted with aspirations for the best outcome. I told myself I'd never tell Mom and Dad about this adventure of learning and acceptance. Richard's assistance was the beginning of a new friendship.

Days passed. Each morning I went in search of a job I desperately needed to support myself. Each evening, I returned to the Men's Home exhausted and discouraged, but there was always a soft knock on my door. I would open it to find Richard offering gentle encouragement and humor, setting me up for the next morning's pursuit.

Sometimes we took my car out for a tour of the city, a snack at a drive-in fast food shop, a conversation. Other evenings I risked letting him in my room to discuss the day's events. Our conversations stayed focused on me. I never learned about his struggles or even the composition of his life in his bare room down the hall. He offered me strength. He became my cheerleader, helping me tackle forward movement and survival. As the days passed and our friendship grew, I automatically left my door open to welcome him in.

After I had been there for a week, the manager told me he could no longer overlook a young woman in their midst and I needed to move on. Luckily, I had secured a job in Hollywood that seemed perfect and glamorous: an assistant for a film company that produced commercials.

The next night, I excitedly told Richard of my success

and invited him to dinner at a nice restaurant, as a form of thanks. His animated facial expression went slack; he shook his head and declined.

"Why?" I asked, feeling hurt.

"We cannot be together—black and white."

After that first night we'd met in the garage, I had not contemplated the issues of difference our skin color might cause. He was just Richard, my new best friend. He was very insistent we not meet again. I had to walk away without ever seeing him again; I never got to know this person of strength and apparent depth. A loss I always regret and have tried to rectify going forward while growing as a person. I even dated a man of color. When I learned about his life challenges, I often thought of Richard.

This journey was only possible by dismissing my fear and taking a chance on Richard, someone I definitely would never have spoken to, let alone received into my world as a friend previously.

Chapter 10

Surrender Gives Happiness with Gratitude

Be content with what you have;
rejoice in the way things are.
When you realize there is nothing lacking,
the whole world belongs to you.

Lao Tzu

Surrender—submitting, yielding and capitulating—is the act of letting go of mental and emotional resistance. But the first thing that comes to my mind is sexual surrender. A friend taught me the meaning of this word when I moved to the West Coast. Previously an uptight lady from the east, I had never learned to surrender. After graduating from college and resettling across the country, I was exposed to a completely different environment. I engaged in my own set of rules: The Hollywood Thing.

It was an exciting time for me. I blossomed into adulthood, a world of color, sounds, and men, so different from what I had experienced under my parent's roof. Now I was settled in my new digs, and these were my people, I was sure.

I struggled after my move, mostly financially, but soon I formed relationships. I encountered the men who wanted my body, not sure why, but I learned how to resist. Sometimes they shamed me for not giving them what they wanted. I was the Holy Grail, the once Virgin Mary, protecting what my parents wished me to protect.

After I was married and pregnant, the challenges with men persisted, even in my work environment. A slimy company vice president propositioned me when I was five months pregnant. I reported his actions to the company president, but this did not positively influence my career. I had to learn how to assert myself in a way they'd understand. I finally got it and gained control.

Then I met Al and became immensely attracted to him. His spirit moved me to the heavens; I was supported by the wings of his being. Our profound feelings for each other never created a future. Sometimes that happens. But he taught me about another kind of surrender, not a sexual one but one that was about giving myself to another, a magical unrestrained submission. He described surrender as emanating from the mind. It allows you to completely give to someone, expansively merging two lives in a way I had never imagined.

An unresolved family issue seemed always present in my mind, draining me emotionally. When traveling through California we stopped at Case De Furitas, a wine gift shop, located in a nowhere agricultural town, surrounded by fields of Bing cherries, strawberries and grapes that Mexicans daily harvested to share the crops' abundance. My sad feelings from this past emotional injury escalated in the store, unique for me because I usually had them under control. I submitted to Al's arms with tears I had held in my heart for years. Together we cried in the middle of the shop, oblivious to anyone for ten minutes. Tourists respectfully went around a twosome entwined. He felt my pain. He cried with me in empathy, joining us forever in that moment. Finally, I understood the word *surrender* he had been attempting to teach me for months. I released my suffering to him; I learned.

It was a magical moment that we never spoke about afterward, but the experience changed my life. That day I understood that someone who cared deeply could support me in releasing my painful trauma. I could risk revealing all to this person. A couple crying in public: this one incident taught me I could share my emotion with another and allowed me to embrace change. I could surrender, any time, any place, with the right person I could trust to help me heal. Over the years, I have thought frequently about the meaning of this moment of surrender, how it happened so comfortably in his arms, how it transformed me.

Surrender does not mean passively putting up with a bad situation. In fact, surrender requires you to stop resisting your discomfort and create a positive flow within yourself (your thoughts and emotions). You allow your feelings to enter your mind, and then you let go of them as you surrender further actions. This plan can eliminate pain and sorrow and create optimistic energy. This is an internal action that requires you to respond and correct an issue in the moment—or let the challenge go forever. It allows you to transcend resistance. Surrender creates a higher vibration healing frequency through acceptance and support.

Releasing to the Universe

Sometimes when you are struggling to find solutions or direction, you can surrender and release your angst to the universe. Communicating with angels daily can reveal a path. Answers surprisingly appear, and they may be very different than you expected.

The key to *uncovering solutions and change* is being open to possibilities. One New Year's Eve, instead of creating goals for the year (fanatically imputing data into an Excel spreadsheet), I found myself drawing a stick figure in gold on a one-by-four-foot piece of discarded paper. I then sprinkled it with glitter and titled it "2014 New Year's Resolutions." My hand continued to draw a curvy black road going down the length of it. Wow, what was that?

The universe told me my path would unfurl as I lived the year. So, I surrendered, gave up all my planning. As a result, I enjoyed my best 365 days ever, tackling the new and frightening with an abundance of joy, noting the milestones along the way on my golden "planner."

Happiness

Along the sacred path, happiness is revealed when each person discovers their true nature, what is important to them and what fulfills them. Happiness is a heightened sense of aliveness that you can attain through physical means or developing a secure sense of self, reaching this point through some form of psychological gratification. Contentment creates pleasure, enjoyment, joy and serenity as you celebrate in the moment.

In the spiritual world, happiness is a natural outcome of being aligned with your essence, your true self. You realize it when fully present in the moment, you feel at peace. Happiness is also about engagement, progressing toward goals that reward with a positive outcome.

You become more creative and attuned with relationships when you live in the moment. As you age, more happiness surfaces, which surprisingly peaks at sixty-five to seventy years of age, according to Sonja Lyubomirsky who wrote about this subject in an AARP magazine article. I don't agree with that number—you can keep reaping the benefits of a higher level of contentment as you mature, find your purpose in life and continue to evolve. We'll see. One theory about why happiness blossoms at sixty-five to seventy years of age is that at this time in their lives, people are more emotionally astute and many spend time with those who make them feel content. There is a shift to realizing what is important in life and that contributes to well-being.

From the recent 2016 World Happiness Report, Denmark is rated as the happiest country in the world. Why? It seems they have relatively simple expectations that are easy to fulfill. Denmark, Switzerland, Iceland and Norway rank highest on the report while the United States is thirteenth. Americans are committed on earning money, having fun and spending time with family. Several African countries are at the bottom of the scale. The life expectancy of many people living in African nations is half that of others who live in more developed countries.

Focusing on what is attainable may be the secret to happiness. Your attitude and how you perceive your world can influence this. People often think that success, health and relationships are all they need to be joyful. These can be taken from you, but not your identity.

The Vedic and Buddhist traditions link five causes to suffering and unhappiness:

- Not knowing your true identity, your essence or true self
- Being unable to change
- Fearing all
- Fearing death
- Identifying with your ego

I have described ego as having a sense of "me," your ideas and your beliefs, but ego is not *who* you are. The ego is based on the voice in your head you have been conditioned to listen to. It is your false self. Your ego is the source of negativity you hear, a statement like "I am not good enough." Actually, when you strip away all labels and ideas, all that is left is *I am*—just your existence. You are what exists, right here and now, as you become self-aware with peace, acceptance, love, compassion, gratitude, kindness, patience, wisdom and strength.

The secret to being content might be to enjoy what you are doing—get lost in it, immerse yourself completely. Listen to your body to tap into your sense of awareness. View your mind and physical being as one force. When they are not synchronized, dysfunction will surface from lack of sleep, a bad diet and stress. When your mind, body and spirit are not in alignment, disharmony is the result.

A great way to connect with your body is to sit, even if it's just for five minutes each day, and bring your thoughts inward as you ground yourself. Soon you become aware of how your body feels, what you need to heal.

You can also listen to your heart-soul. Think and feel from your heart instead of your mind before reacting to a situation; use this feeling of serenity, love and acceptance in the moment as your guide. Daily journal writing can help reveal your emotional states and can direct you to your future.

The best-selling book *The Four Agreements* by Don Miguel identifies four principles for creating happiness in your life:

- Speak with integrity—say only what you mean.
- Don't take anything personally—nothing others say or do is a projection of your reality.
- Don't make assumptions—ask questions and express what you really want.
- Always do your best.

By practicing surrender and living in the moment you

invite happiness into your life. You will achieve personal freedom and release fear and illusions. Your awareness allows you to live with unconditional love, gratitude and respect for yourself and others.

Usually we learn conditional love. We don't respect ourselves. We reject ourselves before others do. We reiterate negative messages that fill our being and poison us. If we are lucky, we learn to practice unconditional love, which strengthens our confidence to make independent decisions uncovering that key. There is no giving to others if we don't respect ourselves. Hopefully someday we learn to fill ourselves with this unconditional acceptance. We create our personal truths and reality. We reject others' control and lies. Inner peace emerges from self-acceptance.

Jungle Hike with a Reward

Some of my happiest moments were preceded by fear and surrender. On an arduous paddle down the Amazon, my guide, Javier, and I became two explorers navigating a difficult frontier. Once logistics were arranged, we pushed off in our canoe along the muddy Amazon to one of its tributaries, the Napo River. We met natives while staying in a secluded village on the shore. We learned about their culture and dined on local fish, berries and palms.

After enduring a strenuous paddle the next day and getting lost on tributaries with little current to help us move through the shallow slow water that had dropped forty-five feet during the dry winter season, we arrived exhausted at one of the few places we didn't sleep under canvas, the remote ExplorNapo Lodge (Acer Lodge).

We unpacked, had a quick dinner and under separate

thatched roofs, fell immediately into a deep slumber. The modest rooms were without electricity, lit only by kerosene lamps, and open to the jungle. Inside were a netted bed and table. The next morning, Javier and I trekked into the dense jungle to find a shaman and learn about his teachings.

Javier had described our long, arduous hike as "just a stroll," possibly true for a man half my age in good physical condition who was used to working his farm in Peru. But not true for me, fifty-five years young taking a respite from desk work at a high-tech company.

We encountered mosquitos, bugs, snakes and even leaches on our path. We sloshed through muck up to our ankles. Vocal monkeys and a variety of birds inhabited the dense canopy. The smoldering heat and humidity were like a sauna. An intense pain clawed my stomach—I had cramps from an intestinal infection. I wanted a bed with clean, crisp sheets, netting for bug protection and a fluffy pillow. I dreamed of a fan gently swirling cool air about my naked body. But with neither bed nor fan in sight, I put one exhausted limb in front of the other, following my protector.

I noticed Javier had his long curved saber knife out of its leather sheath that he constantly wore attached to his waist. He frequently slashed vines to clear our path. I stumbled over the twisted, slippery roots that rose out of the gush of water and decaying vegetation below my boots. We walked for two hours. It was tough, and I was not, but I was becoming so on this difficult one-hundred-mile river trip.

Finally, we arrived at a partial clearing where the sun filtered through the dense, almost impenetrable, jungle growth. The shaman stood directly ahead of us. He was only wearing one thing: a loincloth that covered a minuscule portion of his brown, glistening body.

The next hour was educational and surreal as he showed us around his enchanting garden of plants and vines that had existed in this place for eons—the ReNuPeRu Ethnobotanical Medical Plant Garden. The shaman ferociously guarded this land against loggers who wanted to clear-cut it for financial benefit.

The knowledge of medicinal remedies that had been passed from one generation to the next amazed me. They were priceless. In fact, modern medicine has recently started to recognize the healing properties of his 240 plants, many only found in the Amazon. Often these natural remedies are superior to our "civilized" world of pills.

After this revealing glimpse into an indigenous world, it was time to return to the lodge but both of us were now exhausted, even this superman. Upon arrival, we each found a hammock by an open window and rocked, listening to the sounds of the rainforest.

I slipped in and out of light sleep while looking outside at the shades of parsley-green foliage and savoring the iridescent turquoise-and-black butterflies within our grasp. They moved gracefully, slowly. Lying there with no deadlines and nowhere to go, I completely surrendered to the hammock and the beauty around me. I reached a hypnotic, euphoric state I had never enjoyed before and only now sometimes partake in. I became one with the Amazon.

I tried to understand how I had arrived at that state of submission. I'm not sure, but it had something to do with the physical exertion of hiking, being afraid of the jungle, not to mention that scantily clad native in a far-off part of the world and traveling with a guide I had met over the

Internet. But I had overcome my dread of the unknown to find a place of beauty, a new realm. I was now wrapped in a cocoon of safety, happiness, joy and intense pleasure—because I had surrendered. Maybe, I had found the true meaning of living in the *Now*! But at that time, I didn't understand it or name it as such.

I had a similar joyful experience involving fear and physical exertion with my friend Michael in Costa Rica. This was his first time tackling an international excursion and his baptism to independent traveling. Preceding my arrival, without a plan (not my modus operandi), he found isolated parts of the country, stumbling onto connections with benevolent people who helped him find his way. During one such encounter, he rode to an island in a man-made dugout canoe as huge waves threatened to sink the vessel, but he arrived at his destination, alive and proud of his endeavor.

We met ten days later. I arrived at a town north of San Jose, the Costa Rican capital, and took a bus to meet him in a more intimate city that would be easier for us to navigate, get reacquainted and formulate travel plans. We shared our discoveries as one, both excited to be together. The adventure began.

Toward the end of our trip, situated in a cheap local hotel on the Pacific Coast, Michael and I lounged in the sun, met the community's residents and watched the children play while we enjoyed ceviche with a local beer at a table barely balanced on the sand. We delighted in the scenic view of red-and-blue fishing boats, their paint peeling. Captains maneuvered the boats to shore while the crew repaired their nets for the next day's work.

For us, it was a paradise with no daily plans or expectations, except to relax with fish and beer. But one day we decided it was time for action. Michael had identified a "short, easy" walk for us; why do guys always diminish the challenge?

Wow, that sounded fabulous with all the heat and humidity here. I was glad to be on the move again to find some refreshing, cooler, less salty water. But I had no idea what I'd signed up for. It was not a semi-challenging hike, but a test to survive.

At the outset, I was only able to see the first half of the tall mountain, and nothing resembling water, just a parched, dusty path. Finally, we approached the river, which started out merely as a tiny meandering trickle. As I continued to sweat in the humidity, flies and mosquitoes fed on my partially exposed body. After swatting, trying to cover up and maneuvering to avoid the onslaught of blood-sucking bugs, I calmed my senses and listened to the sounds around me. Maybe we were in a jungle? I was not able to confront that possibility as we moved deeper into the dark, lush vegetation and the sound of insects moving and munching.

Soon the melodies changed to the harsh calls of howler monkeys. I could hear them in the trees directly above as we walked, their low screams alerting all in the vicinity that humans were invading their territory. They weren't the meek creatures you might imagine holding in your arms, taking home to bed to cuddle. No, when I passed beneath them, I imagined predators that would defend their homes and family with sharp incisors, evident as they opened their mouths with each screech.

Now I know a bit more about these monkeys. Weighing up to twenty pounds, they are the largest of the new world monkeys but not the enormous size I visualized when hearing their throaty, terrifying sounds. Fairly peaceful vegetarians, they have declined fifty percent in the last fifteen years due to deforestation, which has resulted from additional road construction, probably for loggers.

On our hike, I didn't know any of those details. All I knew was that we were innocently intruding on their space in order to glimpse water splashing down a rugged cliff. It was surprisingly unnerving to be on the monkey's turf without knowing anything about their behavior or carrying any weapons for protection.

Michael seemed to pay no attention. Was he pretending or did the primates just not worry him? Once more I was with a man that was years younger and more fit than I was. *It does make a difference in your agility and endurance to be older,* I kept telling myself, but I did my best to keep up with him or I'd be left with these primates. I soon realized he would not slow down for the woman behind. Michael had a theory. On the highway you "push" a car in front of you when a driver is moving too slowly by approaching closer and closer. Maybe he was trying to "pull" me forward with his fast hiking.

Soon the terrain changed. We climbed over insignificant slippery rocks along the river that grew into medium-sized rocks and then enormous boulders that I needed to pull myself up and over. Occasionally Michael stopped with a deep breath of resignation, waited for me and offered his muscular hand to help me over obstacles on the path.

In the heat and humidity, and considering my ripe young age of sixty-three, this hike was definitely beyond my skill level. I was slowing down, but the carrot of a waterfall was dangling in front of me and motivating me to keep going. I always craved hikes to view falls. I could practically feel the invigorating water spray in this steamy environment. I moved forward.

The incline leveled a bit. No longer concerned about the howlers, I could hear water roaring above, but I couldn't see it.

Oh No. I paused a few minutes and looked up—a steep mountain of clay mud with no end in sight. In front of us was a ribbon-thin waterfall fed from a trickle of water falling from above. Had we arrived? At that point, I hadn't heard of the *three* waterfall climb, but Michael had.

I hesitantly said, "Are we here? This is wonderful, let's swim."

All I heard, as I often did in our relationship, was an emphatic "No." Without hesitating, he continued to climb toward the heavens. What could I to do? Stay with the bugs chewing on my body, with the animals that surrounded us, or follow him?

After defiantly sitting on a rock and refusing to budge, I gave into fear. I rose and climbed upward, trying to catch the man who never slowed. It wasn't easy. My feet slipped on the rust-colored dirt and the 60 percent incline was impossible to navigate unless you grabbed onto the vines and tree roots, which stained my fingers.

My clothes were saturated with perspiration. Might my lungs explode? I could barely breathe as I attempted to keep up with this man. Finally, we reached a plateau and he stopped. *Yahoo*! I made it. Proudly, I glanced at the pool below waterfall number two.

We panted. He offered me a drink of his water. This hadn't been so bad—we, well I, had survived this little *stroll*. Neither of us spoke, our strength spent. My heart finally slowed to a normal rate, almost to the point of

Three waterfall "stroll"

enjoying our high vista; we were precariously perched on a rock a short distance above the clouds.

Incredibly, he kept moving up a steeper mountain wall. I contemplated murder. *That's not nice.* How the heck could he do that to me, not even asking if I would go to heaven with him, straight up?

I was fuming, exhausted and contemplating what I always contemplate when I'm with him. Should I turn back, accept defeat at not accomplishing *his* goal? Or should I keep going to what could be nirvana, as we often found, persevere through what hopefully would be our last assault on a mountain that didn't seem to end in altitude?

How could I give up striving, racing after this man I was fiercely attached to? That was certainly not in my ability at that time. I always wanted more of life, more of him. So somehow I found an ounce of vitality—while vowing in the future to work out a bit more diligently at the gym—and put one wobbly leg in front of the other.

Exhausted, barely able to move forward and constantly slipping dangerously backward, we continued. He noticed with a sixth sense—never turning in my direction—when to stop and reach downward for my upstretched hand. He'd stop my slippage and pull me toward his body. Up, up, up, until we reached paradise.

The mountaintop. We took a long five minutes to enjoy the vista, to celebrate looking down at where we had come from and to drink water with an unquenchable thirst. The ordeal was now over; we had made it to the pinnacle and I enjoyed a moment of celebration for me.

But suddenly Michael disappeared over the cliff. I turned to see him standing below me, opposite from where we had ascended. He had a triumphant smile on his face. Why? Soon I realized I had not completed our mission. I would need to rappel down a rope, barely attached by other adventurers, to the blissful waterfall pool fifty feet below.

Michael dangled an almost empty water bottle that appeared precious as gold. To quench my boundless thirst, would I need to follow? I had never repelled. It seemed my struggle on this hike would not end.

Surprisingly, I didn't take long to decide what to do. Now into this quest, I expertly slid down the rope to reach my reward below, a thundering waterfall and my man. Three feet before I hit the dusty ground, his unyielding hands expertly grabbed my waist and gently lowered me to the ground. A long, lush kiss followed, maybe one of recognition that I had persevered and was now equal to him.

I was pooped, but I still felt such intense feelings for him; pride with gratitude surfaced. I had succumbed to his desired goal. We now jumped into this pure blue river of the gods and joyously swam, finding a perfect cove behind the cool wash, our bliss together.

This prize took lots of effort. I had to conquer some of my fears—being alone on the trail with threatening animals nearby and feeling uncertain that I could mount this precipice. I knew Michael would always be watching, but a bit ahead of me. With this bond, I guess sometimes you surrender to the other's wishes, allowing that person to achieve, sometimes on their own and sometimes with you. When they're in need, you assist and celebrate as one.

Is this what happiness is composed of?

Spiritual Survival in the Desert Creates Gratitude

I read an interesting story on the Internet about a woman named Ann Rodgers. She was from a military family who created art and practiced Reiki therapy. Could you survive nine days in the winter desert of Arizona with that background? Her misguided trip to surprise her daughter and celebrate her own birthday and her grandson's never materialized as planned.

A survivalist, she packed plenty of food and water for her trip, a short two-hour drive from Tucson to Phoenix. However, she made two big mistakes. First, she told no one of her travel plans. In search of fuel for her hybrid Ford Fusion, she took a wrong turn, got lost driving on a dusty path as her car sputtered on zero and then stopped in no man's land of the White Mountains in Eastern Arizona. There was no one in sight. Frightened, she had nowhere to go for help.

Ann had two treasured animals with her, her two-year-old rescue Queensland terrier mix, Queenie, and her cat, Nike. At night, during frigid temperatures, she cuddled in her car with the animals, covering them and herself with the extra clothes and blankets stored in her trunk. She shared her food and water with her animals.

Climbing several ridges to find cell phone coverage, she used her binoculars to survey the terrain from the mountaintop. But she could not see civilization or even a path leading to somewhere. She did locate, at the bottom of one of the canyons, a stream. Her cell battery low, she was barely able to text a friend, Bruce Trees, and tell him that she was marooned in the desert. He never heard from her again, because soon her battery died.

Bruce, a retired marine and a man of action, fortunately

called the local authorities. But after three days, no one had found Ann. She was down to one protein bar and had a limited amount of water. Exhausted, she considered her options. Survival classes advise you to remain with your vehicle, so her second survival mistake could have killed her. She decided the time had come for action and she left her car.

Ann packed a bag containing sketching tools, paper, a jar of water, a protein bar, a lighter, a knife and a few clothes. She left a message in her car explaining she was out of gas and food and was moving south. It was difficult, but she decided to leave her cat in the car—he would be the least able to survive the journey—and then headed down the canyon to find water.

The day after Bruce's call, a detective at the Gila County Sheriff's office received a request from the Fort Apache Indian Reservation. They needed help searching for a lady whose car they had found with a very ravenous cat inside. Men with dogs found tracks in the sandy silt. After four days in this environment, they suspected it might be a recovery operation.

Ann moved southwest in the hopes of finding a warmer climate. Queenie always ventured ahead, creating a path on the desert floor and discovering the safest place to cross rivers. Ann followed. She celebrated her birthday by waking to a hummingbird's wings in her face. She contemplated its beauty, surrendered to it, as the sun started to warm the earth and welcome one more day on the desert floor. She felt joy, until the reality of her current circumstance surfaced. She screamed and swore in frustration. Her unheard message echoed back to her, as if to say, "You are on your own babe, save yourself."

Her birthday gift appeared as a slow-moving turtle in a

murky pond—protein. She captured it in the frigid water and killed it with a knife. She cooked the turtle in its shell and ate it immediately, which helped her exist a bit longer.

Due to her unwavering spiritual beliefs, survival training, knowledge of Reiki (an energy force from a higher power that resides within us) and her connection to nature, Ann had the tools to assist in her survival. They gave her confidence that she could cope with this ordeal. From childhood, she had spent most of her time outdoors hiking, learning about the power of herbs and practicing subsistence skills that enabled her to identify edible plants. These skills were helpful, but she was losing energy fast. And Queenie seemed so famished she found clover to eat.

They found a pond and then spring water to fill the jar Ann carried. At night she built fires, starting them with paper from her sketch pad and a cigarette lighter. She became concerned she might run out of fuel, so she started carrying hot embers in moss during the day's walk to start her next evening fire, as Indians have done for centuries. Enduring below-freezing temperatures, she shared her red satchel at night with her dog. They alternated using it for warmth and a buffer against the freezing ground. During a thunderstorm, they took shelter in a cave, building a fire for the night, one of many sites searchers uncovered as they tracked their footprints.

Ann was doing the best she could to stay alive. She left a distress signal, using bleached elk bones and stones to spell out *Help*. She built many fires during her ordeal but eventually got a helicopter's attention with a signal fire. Ann frantically fanned the flames when she heard the plane overhead, and they saw her sign. She was not ready to give up on life yet.

On April 9, after nine days of being lost, a tribal game

and forest officer found Queenie walking out of Canyon Creek. They feared the worst. A dog without its mistress could be a severe problem. But fifteen minutes later, they located Ann waving her big red bag with all the power she had left.

Ann suffered from exposure, but surprisingly she was still alive after these challenging days. Crying and praising those who had found her, she offered words of gratitude. This woman happened to be seventy-two, not the age of your typical survivor. Raised as a Congregationalist, Ann would not give up on life as she surrendered to her situation. Through her faith, she was able to dismiss despair and find hope and beauty each day of the journey. That may have saved her life.

"Because we age, wisdom [and] memories become part of your knowledge base that help you survive," Ann said. She gave blessings for her incredible environment on this long ordeal—inspired by dramatic canyons, trees and rocks that sustained the life of her and her dog. She labeled it her spiritual journey. Possibly the prayers of her church played a role in why this woman lived. Her survival was a feat expert say most would find impossible due to the dangers of hypothermia in the cold and rain. She thanked her God.

Chapter 11

New Beginnings

*Just when the caterpillar thought
the world was over, it became a butterfly.*

English Proverb

Growth

WITHOUT MOVING FORWARD, A JOURNEY ENDS IN stagnation. Many people are unhappy with their lives, have unfilled desires and are not searching for how to change.

Consciously deciding how to explore your future and uncovering what is important to you can make all the difference in directing your growth. Awakening as a spiritual being, you learn to live in the moment, eliminate suffering by dismissing yesterday and tomorrow. You get lost in the moment, involved completely; this is the secret to enjoyment and harmony. This energy nurtures and lifts you beyond the physical world and often imparts clarity, compassion, gratitude, kindness, wisdom, strength, courage, love, loyalty and faith. You found your soul, the core of your being. You are at peace.

It takes vision, learning and old-fashioned persistence to alter deep-rooted behaviors, and you should be proud of each step along this path. As you grow, it is surprising to look back to where you started and celebrate the *you* of today. You've influenced others in a positive way and acquired wisdom.

A journal can help you measure your goals and successes. As you review your progress, you may be surprised. Each year I assess endeavors and celebrate the amazing path set before me. This road to uncovering my higher self and power has infused me with a new persona—a gentler, kinder, more benevolent and conscious person over time.

Thirty years ago, a boyfriend started me on this important quest by asking, "What is life all about? What is its meaning?" I was young, in my early forties, when I heard these words I barely understood, but I met the challenge to find answers. I searched and within a few days I had found *my* meaning of life:

- To love and be loved.
- To contribute to society—creatively, supportively.
- To assist with our environment's survival, helping any way I can.

With time and maturity, I added one more:

- To ascend to a higher spiritual level through my daily practice as a healer and conduit.

When I wrote down my meaning of life, it was easy and came to me very quickly. I reported back to my boyfriend, and he seemed impressed. I realize now that I found my essence at a relatively young age. It directed me through a life of wonder, using those goals to provide my framework for living.

In the past, I needed to protect my boundaries, which were often abused by others. Although difficult, I found my grit and wrote the following, which guided me to this moment. I review it many times when I seem to forget.

My Pledge

July 7, 1998

Today I begin to honor myself, control my destiny, chart my path and move in that direction. I will take full responsibility for my happiness and fulfillment, creating what I want as my legacy. I will do this in the following way:

- I will awake to the dawn unfolding outside my window and appreciate its beauty, sounds and scents. Meditation will ground me. I will remember who I am, the positive growth I've accomplished, and review my life priorities to help shape and direct the day.
- I am powerful, compassionate and accomplished—my desire is to enrich and enjoy beauty, interact with others and to find joy in daily living. I will repeal negative behavior and only drink from the well of good in others.
- I will think positively during my days' encounters and offer my caring to others. I will take time to watch a spider spin its masterpiece of silk and to laugh at a squirrel racing exuberantly toward an adjacent tree as it loses its balance, tumbling and then regaining its stride and scurrying ever upward.
- And last, I release anger from my life, the blaming that is negative and poisonous.

My meaning of life along with my pledge became the basis for writing my mission statement.

My Mission Statement:

To contribute to our world with compassion and creativity through peace and love while honoring my passions and self first:

- I will contribute to society and our environment with my creativity and caring.
- I will be loyal, honest, self-confident and approachable.
- I will pursue my passions of cultural diversity and travel.
- I will first honor myself.
- I desire peace, acceptance and the giving and receiving of love.
- I will never lower my standards or ignore my family, physical well-being or personal goals.

My discovery of who I am and what is right for me today stems from these words, along with my most important statement, *I will first honor myself.* It took me years to feel I earned the right to assert this statement, which should be your birthright.

You can try this exercise. In one line, sum up who you are and what you wish to strive for, your life purpose. Follow this line with goals that support your purpose. This mission statement is your bare essence in life revealed; it's you discovering your passions.

This statement emerges from deep within. It should be short and that is not easy. When I created mine years ago, I rewrote it multiple times, and each time it became more concise until I had the core of my beliefs. Not everyone will do this in the same way, but my format is easy to remember and has guided me during my years of growth.

One of my favorite motivators is Wayne Dyer, a philosopher who combined new thought self-actualization theory and nondenominational spirituality. Each time I heard or saw him speak, my self-development exploded.

His teachings promote infinite intelligence through the god or spirit that resides within each person and selfless acts to assist and heal. Loving unconditionally and teaching others is a milestone of this belief system. His emphasis on harnessing personal power and healing self and others, with the aid of your life forces—that vitality of energies within—now influence my living.

Dyer suggests that if you change the way you look at things, the things you look at change. The way we conduct our lives reflects our perception so when we are positive, an outcome of an event is also likely to be the same. You can Google his quotes for inspiration and they often become daily affirmations of mine.

Dyer is one more person who has assisted in my growth. It is often much easier to just continue conducting your life as you have in the past. Change is frightening, and often you need a burning desire to move in a new direction. Sometimes you hit bottom, sometimes you see your time rapidly eroding with no meaning as you age and sometimes—it is just your time.

How do you change?

Remember, your imagination has no limits; it takes you anywhere, anytime. All is possible, if you believe it. Visualization is an amazingly powerful tool. Daily visualize what you wish for, not what was, and it will be yours. Everything that exists, someone imagined. With that spark, what you desire grows to be a great light of reality—aim for the extraordinary, never the ordinary.

Phrase your thoughts and sentences with the words *I am* and *I will attract* (what you want in your life). Don't allow negatives into internal or external conversations. Your feelings create your destiny. Live as if what you want already exists.

One of my practices during the last five minutes before falling asleep is to review the positives of my day, saying, "I am . . ." This seals encouraging feelings in your memory and sets your intention for the next day. For example, after spending time with a person who was in a difficult situation, I listened, offered support and helped guide her toward a new and enriched outcome. I did this with pure love and when we parted, I could see a new joy reflected in her face. That night I said, "I am love," which reminded me of that day's experience of helping another. When I awoke, this was the first thing I remembered, and it directed me toward a fulfilling day.

Balance

I was a bit crazed. I had deadlines to meet for my book, for my friends and for a building project. How to fit it all in?

My answer was to stop my yoga, meditation and exercise program. I would not need friends, not now with all my deadlines. Late nights would make it all work. I'd rise at 7:00 am and go to bed at midnight. I would also give up my beloved photography. That would allow me to save time.

Wrong.

None of this became my solution. All of my passions needed to be integrated into my existence, not just a few.

I was off-balance, cranky and exhausted. I even had heart palpitations. I'd had these feelings before during my high-tech years as a project manager for a high-profile Internet security company. It was a demanding job with sixty-hour workweeks, sometimes more. Flying to unusual parts of the world to launch products left me with little personal time and a boatload of stress.

I maintained this hectic pace for some time, but eventually I grew numb, became lethargic, got little rest and had no time for personal connections. My physical workout routine became nonexistent. Only work was left, and I became a linear, fixated machine.

One day, I was working on a detailed spreadsheet of tasks for the next day, next week and next month when I stopped. Pain stung my arm, creating havoc and discomfort in my chest. My heart was racing, to where I knew not. At that moment, I could think clearly about life, about what I wanted and what I did not want. Emphatically, I *did not want* to die at this laminated desk staring at a pulsating computer screen.

Driving home from work that day, I suddenly saw my unbalanced life, what I longed for and why I drove to the mountains or to the country when I could no longer stand the person I had become: a shell, devoid of emotion as I pushed myself, my being, my humanity, my passion, my essence, so I could get all my projects done. On those three-day extended weekends away from work, I did not acknowledge my true objective: make myself human again.

I've learned that health and happiness come from a balance of activities and a healthy dose of downtime. While striving to reach goals, you can easily get off track. If you're lucky and you've learned the right lessons in the past, you eventually wake up to your craziness. Something alerts you if you pay attention. Your heath, vivaciousness, friends and family suffer when your life is out of balance. Sometimes you have to go back to the basics or create balance for the first time.

I had no desire to be that person again. Something had to give before I crumbled. I would reassess, make changes and start living again fully. During my previous time of unbalance, I began discovering who I truly was. When striving for a current goal, sometimes I forgot my lessons and piled too much on my agenda. I needed to stop, correct and redirect my behavior.

So, even after you have found the answers and changed, it is always possible to slip back into negative past behaviors.

If you are stressed and sick, you may need to examine your life, your schedule and your motives. It's a time for honesty. Are you driven by fear—maybe that no one else is capable of doing the job right but you? Possibly, your self-esteem is low, and you feel the need to accomplish more to be appreciated.

It's up to you to discover the meaning of *your* life as you identify who you are and who you will be. Once I uncovered my life purpose, it became a subconscious push to keep me committed to what I am passionate about. Of course, sometimes I still try too hard to accomplish something. I tune in to those negative feeling and know I must rebalance.

How do you rebalance?

One way is first to define your personal priorities, your vital obligations, that you need to achieve well-being and satisfaction—maybe work, exercise or meditation? You put them in order of importance or assign them a percentage of your day's attention.

Your second list contains activities that are not crucial to your passion or the meaning of your life. You may need to say no to some of these, request help in getting them accomplished or delegate responsibilities. These are not vital obligations.

Thus, you have a framework, along with knowing what your purpose in life is, that excites and brings you joy. It's your connection to your internal soul. If you can make choices according to this framework, you can regain your equilibrium and feel whole. You do not have to accept living a life that is fractured into meaningless pieces. You can achieve an evolution of your consciousness.

Just as it's important to make wise choices about what you spend your time doing, it's also important to reward yourself. Create a pleasure list. Some of my items are taking a walk in the rain, enjoying a cup of coffee, writing in my journal, lighting candles, dancing to an addictive beat or relaxing to soft music.

Once you have found your balance, you'll know. Living a balanced life contributes to joy, peace and happiness. Relishing this sense of balance allows me to fulfill one of my missions: to find my higher power, to be all that I can. My angels and higher spirit seem to work through me, when I listen, allowing me to support others as a conduit. I have learned my touch can move the energy from our universe, heal myself and others. It is my contribution in life as I continue to learn about spirituality.

Living Fearlessly

For me, living this way has been a source of great enjoyment and has paid huge dividends. When you risk, you reap rewards and opportunities you would never otherwise find. You move through life with zest and flourish, with satisfaction and meaning.

You deserve to uncover your best self without judgment, through unconditional love. It's your entitlement, even more fundamental than happiness and transformation,

Challenging the waves

according to *The Book of Joy* by the Dalai Lama, Archbishop Desmond Tutu and Douglas Abrams.

When young I contemplated terminating my existence as I suffered teen conflicts, such as the end of an important relationship. I often think what I would have given up if I'd gone through with it. It is painful for me to even consider that I might have committed this act. I would have lost the beautiful child gifted to me who has become my best friend. We each face our own life struggles independently and then reconnect, to become one. I've been blessed with the pleasure of spoiling two unique granddaughters.

Abundance consumes my path as I offer gratitude. I have become an independent, creative contributor to women's empowerment, art and my self-help mission. It has shaped me into the person I am today. What I give and receive daily makes me cry though the practices I have found with teachers, including friends, who became my caring guides.

Suicide, this destructive act, contemplated during my youth of frustration, would have been a waste as I now view it from my blossoming existence. I guess reflecting on this possible wrong turn makes my gratitude even more poignant.

Through the words I share with you—a window into my pain, joy and discoveries—I distill this world of mine to where I now think from my heart and acknowledge my and other's emotions with empathy and forgiveness. I have become a gentler, more connected person, consumed with happiness, pure bliss most days, and content living in the cosmos of serenity with thankfulness. This gift is possible for you.

As I emerge from my cocoon and become a lovely butterfly, I am ever reminded of my granddaughter's words,

"You are beautiful—inside and out." Her words are a daily reminder I partially believe, but with time will fully accept. That is the essence of unconditional love.

Supporting Others

One of the most meaningful gifts we give others or receive is support, which is derived from our caring.

I had a friend, an ex-lover, who challenged the borders of normalcy. He was mine for multiple years. We shared our passion of nature and the outdoors and pursued personal adventures as one. Eventually, our experiences became weird, dangerous. I was no longer able to go on his "journeys." I shriveled and nearly died—but he actually did.

I spent time meditating, trying to rectify the non-rectifiable event. I found my courage to move on, recreate life with many new goals. I learned that you never reject another person—despite the pain they cause—because you do not completely understand their world or struggle for recovery, and you should be there for them. This is what having compassion means.

I now respect other people's limits, whether constructed by themselves or their families. No longer do I judge. Instead I encourage and befriend others' efforts, successful or not. The world should not judge our outcomes, only we get to do that. You support a person, no matter what they do to you, with boundaries.

I currently align with and assist my family members, boyfriends, girlfriends and mankind. It could be a stranger on the street who needs a smile or a special word of acknowledgment. It could be a dejected doggie needing a pet, a friend facing challenges or a close relative struggling through a financial debacle. Providing a key to resolve the small difficulties in life creates a sense of connection, allowing others to heal in a small way. It is my contribution in life. I believe that what may appear as an insignificant act compounds and produces healing.

Life happens.

What are you looking for in your spirituality? One person's answer may sum it up. She searches for peace, solutions to her life questions and inspiration. A light that emanates from within, along with your intelligence, produces this magical ability to creatively construct what you wish to enjoy in this lifetime and to support our planet's inhabitants.

When life changes are offered, you must first acknowledge their presence and challenges as you learn new concepts. You revise familiar patterns, discover new ones and, finally, embrace a new direction.

My ardent link with the spiritual world is through nature. What is yours? If you have not found that answer, begin your search and reap its rewards while discovering purpose and your unique higher power.

From where I stand, the culmination of my life, all the lessons and experiences, creates who and why I am today. My brand of spirituality reveals itself and defines me well. We are all unique personas, just as our beliefs and practices are diverse.

People need love and a shared sense of spirit. My hope for our human race is to understand we are all connected beings, that we should explore, learn and grow with that in mind. Imagine a world where love and spirituality prevail, a wish for the future.

I am blessed as a spiritual traveler to have harmony and a yearning to help others at this time in my life.

I learn.

Frost on my window — who is the spiritual creator?

Namaste

*Every day, think as you wake up, today I
am fortunate to be woken up.
I am alive. I have a precious human
life. I am not going to waste it.
I am going to use all of my energies to develop myself,
to expand my heart out to others, to achieve
enlightenment for the benefit of all beings.
I am going to have kind thoughts toward others.
I am not going to get angry or think badly about others.
I am going to benefit others
as much as I can.*

Dalai Lama XIV

Acknowledgments

WITH THE CLOSURE OF ONE MORE QUEST, I WISH TO THANK those who have carried me along this path.

Through the voices of wisdom and compassion, family, friends and acquaintances, my team of editors and designers, have helped me understand my discoveries which create my soul. One person stands out by her unselfish act to assist at the last minute, Michelle Harris, who was recruited to be a first reader and a wonderful source of grammar, proofing and suggestions of clarity.

Special thanks to Leilani Busbin for sharing the art on my back cover. Leilani has been an energetic healer for over twenty-five years. Creativity in the form of art has been a healing pursuit for her. The art is inspired and channeled by a spirit guide. She starts with a blank canvas and no preconceived design. The spirits produce her art. "I make art to show my soul I am listening." Pat Wiederspan Jones once stated. You can purchase or learn more about Busbin's acrylic and watercolor art by contacting: leilani4444@gmail.com.

I would also give my gratitude to Kit Cummings who made himself available for our conversations and assistance on spirituality and world peace I've tapped for this book. You can follow his wonderful projects at: http://kitcummings.com/about-kit/

The gifts from the universe have moved me to find courage and explore new avenues of daily joys. With this knowledge, I share what I've learned with my readers, available for all to grow. My wish is for a community of the world to celebrate and unite in their spirituality. With complete gratitude, I continue along this road.

My Research

Introduction
The Awakening

Barna Group. "Millennials at Church: What Millennials Want When They Visit Church." March 4, 2015. www.barna.com/research/what-millennials-want-when-they-visit-church/.

Beliefnet.com. "Baby Boomers, Shopping For Faith." Accessed May 1, 2017. www.beliefnet.com/wellness/2006/10/baby-boomers-shopping-for-faith.aspx.

Masci, David and Michael Lipka. "Americans May Be Getting Less Religious, But Feelings of Spirituality Are on the Rise." Pew Research Center. January 21, 2016. www.pewresearch.org/fact-tank/2016/01/21/americans-spirituality/.

Chapter 2
Religion and Belief Systems

Anderson, Jeff. "Living with Purpose: Learning From Regrets of the Dying." *A Place for Mom Newsletter*, posted January 19, 2016. www.aplaceformom.com/blog/11-20-13learning-from-regrets-of-dying/.

Brumley, Linda. *Hand in Hand with God: Finding Your Path to Forgiveness*. Spring, TX: Illumination Publishers, 2014.

Cummings, Kit. *Peace Behind The Wire: A Nonviolent Resolution*. Alpharetta, GA: Booklogix, 2015.

Davchevski, Dejan. "7 Differences Between Religion and Spirituality." TheOpenMind.com. November 24, 2014. www.the-open-mind.com/7-differences-between-religion-and-spirituality-1/.

Grant, Tobin. "The Great Decline: 60 Years of Religion in One Graph." *Religion News Service.* January 27, 2014. religionnews.com/2014/01/27/great-decline-religion-united-states-one-graph/.

Green, Emma. "It's Hard to Go to Church." *The Atlantic.* August 23, 2016. www.theatlantic.com/politics/archive/2016/08/religious-participation-survey/496940/.

Helliwell, John F., Haifang Huang, and Shun Wang, eds. "The Geography of World Happiness," in *World Happiness Report 2015,* edited by John F. Helliwell, Richard Layard, and Jeffrey Sachs, 12-41. New York: Sustainable Development Solutions Network, 2015. worldhappiness.report/wp-content/uploads/sites/2/2015/04/WHR15.pdf.

Power of Peace Project. Accessed March 30, 2015. Powerofpeaceproject.com.

ReligionFacts.com. "The Big Religion Chart." Last modified November 21, 2016. www.religionfacts.com/big-religion-chart.

WGBH Educational Foundation. "Religion: Three Religions, One God." Accessed February 15, 2017. www.pbs.org/wgbh/globalconnections/mideast/themes/religion/.

Young, J. Gareth. "Kit Cummings: The Power of Peace." March 30, 2015. garethjyoung.com/kit-cummings/.

Chapter 4
Death and Living with Purpose

Hammerschlag, Carl A. *The Dancing Healers: A Doctor's Journey of Healing with Native Americans.* New York: HarperCollins, 2011.

Chapter 5
Vision Quest

Bodhishantra. "The Story of My Vision Quest." August 8, 2009. www.paulchefurka.ca/VisionquestStory.html.

Circles of Air & Stone. "What Is a Vision Quest?" Accessed April 1, 2017. www.questforvision.com/programs/vision-quest/what-is-a-vision-quest/.

Crystalinks.com. "Vision Quest." Accessed April 1, 2017. www.crystalinks.com/visionquest.html.

Krown, Maddisen K. "What Is a Vision Quest and Why Do One?" Ask Maddisen (blog). July 19, 2009. www.huffingtonpost.com/maddisen-k-krown/ask-maddisen-what-is-a-vi_b_217432.html.

School of Lost Borders. "Vision Quests." Accessed 3-6-17. schooloflostborders.org/.

Chapter 7
The Now

Hebért, Michele. *The Tenth Door: An Adventure Through the Jungles of Enlightenment.* Austin, Emerald Book Company, 2011.

Kurus Mary. "A Beginner's Guide to Energy Terminology: Energy Fields and Energy Symbols." Accessed 4-1-17. www.mkprojects.com/beginners-guide-energy-terminology.

Tolle, Eckhart. *The Power of Now: A Guide to Spiritual Enlightenment.* Vancouver, BC: Namaste Publishing, 2004.

Schucman, Helen. *A Course in Miracles.* Mill Valley, CA: Foundation for Inner Peace, 1995.

Ruiz, Don Miguel. *The Four Agreements.* San Rafael: Amber-Allen Publishing, 1997.

Makransky, John. "Awakening Through Love." Online Seminar, Science of Meditation, Self-Help, and Compassion Forum from Shambhala Mountain, May 26, 2017.

Physicsforums.com. "Does a Rock Have Energy?" Last modified June 7, 2007. www.physicsforums.com/threads/does-a-rock-have-.173133/.

Chapter 8
Love, What Binds and Makes Us Human

Burton, Neel. "These Are the 7 Types of Love." *Psychology Today*. June 25, 2016. www.psychologytoday.com/blog/hide-and-seek/201606/these-are-the-7-types-love.

Chapter 9
Fear

Rankin, Lissa. *The Fear Cure: Cultivating Courage as Medicine for the Body, Mind, and Soul*. Carlsbad: Hay House, 2015.

Chapter 10
Surrender Gives Happiness with Gratitude

Helliwell, John F., Haifang Huang, and Shun Wang, eds. "The Distribution of World Happiness," in *World Happiness Report 2016*, edited by John F. Helliwell, Richard Layard, and Jeffrey Sachs, 12-41. New York: Sustainable Development Solutions Network, 2016.

Stern, Ray. "Tucson Woman Describes How She Survived Nine Days in Arizona Wilderness." *Phoenix New Times*. April 13, 2016. www.phoenixnewtimes.com/news/tucson-woman-describes-how-she-survived-nine-days-in-arizona-wilderness-exclusive-8212920.

Chapter 11
New Beginnings

Lama, Dalai, Archbishop Desmond Tutu, and Douglas Carlton Abrams. *The Book of Joy*. New York: Random House, 2016.

About the Author

SALLY DEMASI grew up in New York, earned a bachelor of science and studied abroad in Siena, Italy. Upon graduating, she struck out for California in search of adventures.

After her stint in the California high-tech industry, she found her life home in the small, pristine town of McCall, Idaho, where she now rafts, kayaks, camps and skis. She is free to discover her love of writing and photography in nature.

DeMasi is the author of *Courage Quest*, a book that encourages others to bolster their courage and enjoy a positive self-image. The book details her solo international travels, her exploration of other cultures and how she conquers her fears.

Her second book, *Survival Quest*, explores true stories about overcoming physical and emotional crisis through encounters with the spiritual realm, emotional support, physical preparedness and fate.

This book, *Spiritual Quest*, is a culmination of her past quests. It describes her very personal search to uncover a life purpose and reveals how to find your higher spiritual self.

Her photos appear in exhibits, books, newspapers and upscale galleries as well as on her blogs. A versatile artist, she explores new territory through creating vibrant impressions.

Contact Sally

Your questions and comments are welcome!

E-mail: sallydemasi4@gmail.com
Phone: (208) 866-6218

Visit Sally's website and blogs to learn
more about her books and photographs:

sallydemasi4.wixsite.com/quest
(overview of quest books, photos)

www.couragequest.net
(book and courage information)

www.SurvivalSpiritualQuest.com
(books and survival, spiritual information)

www.sallydemasi.com
(photos)

www.ingramcontent.com/pod-product-compliance
Lightning Source LLC
Chambersburg PA
CBHW071305110426
42743CB00042B/1181